T0147913

BENJAMIN!

A RAVENOUS WOLF

- REVISED EDITION -

JANET L. RUSSELL

Order this book online at www.trafford.com
or email orders@trafford.com

Most Trafford titles are also available at major online book retailers.

Mrs. Janet Russell
P.O. Box H-45043
Hunters, Grand Bahama
E-mail: jlouise5544@hotmail.com

Printed in the United States of America.

ISBN: 978-1-4669-6946-9 (sc)
ISBN: 978-1-4669-6945-2 (e)

Trafford rev. 01/03/2013

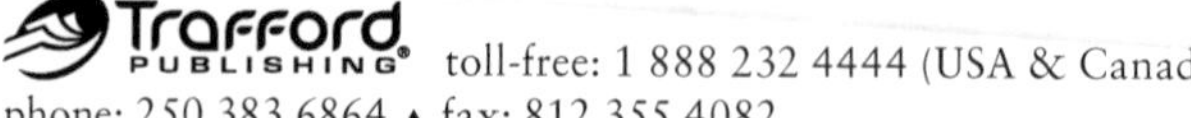

toll-free: 1 888 232 4444 (USA & Canada)
phone: 250 383 6864 • fax: 812 355 4082

Contents

PROPHETIC DECLARATIONS

A Season of Birthing

We have gone through a season of Birthing as the Body of Christ.

Before every great move of God, the People of God go through much pain and struggle to bring forth the power of God into this Earth's realm

Many within the body of Jesus Christ after going through the desired process of becoming 'heirs of God, and joint-heirs with Christ;' should expect to also suffer as He did. Rachael in this story during the nine months of gestation and delivery, suffered so much sorrow that when she gave birth to Benjamin she named him "Ben Oni, Son of my sorrow", she died never understanding that her (child) ministry would bring total glory to God.

Jacob named His son, "Benjamin, Son of my right hand", that which was familiar to him, a (Child) ministry he was capable of producing and promoting, one in which he functioned and was sure to be successfully administered. A (child) ministry that did not bring glory to God, but glory to 'himself', he being labeled a trickster and a deceiver, passed on to his son an inheritance of his own personality.

During the latter years of Jacobs's life, his name now changes to Israel,[1] he blessed his sons, and as he blesses Benjamin, He said:

[1] Israel: ". . . *for as a prince hast thou power with God and with men, and hast prevailed." Genesis 33:28 (NIV)*

"Benjamin is a ravenous wolf; in the morning he devours the prey, in the evening he divides the plunder.

The Bride of Christ who is called in her hour to bring forth the power of the Almighty God, those who are only interested in obtaining status with their own selfish motives and desires, will also in this hour labor to bring forth (A child) ministries after their own kind, ministries that will be called ravenous wolves.

Those who follow after the heart of God and seek an intimate relationship with Him will bring forth (child) ministries after His kind.

PART ONE

Giving Birth

Introduction

A garden enclosed is my sister,
My Spouse!
A spring shut up, a fountain sealed,

Awake, O north wind; and come, thou south wind;
Blow upon my garden,
That the spices thereof may flow out
Let my beloved come into His garden
And taste His pleasant fruits
Solomon's Song 4:12, 16

The Song of Solomon is a beautiful scene of our Lord Jesus and His bride, the Church. Throughout the many illustrations, the bride groom is drawing his future bride out of herself and into an intimate relationship with Him.

In this featured passage, the bride, who at the onset of this relationship refuses to open up and be exposed to the emotional imbalance that cripples her, capturing her sense of growth and her ability to communicate her insecurities to Him. He has visited her on many occasions, but on this visit, through the encouragement of the love she had discovered in Him and His dealings with her through a period of time, He finally achieves His goal.

He awakens her emotions by allowing the strong north winds of harsh conditions, disappointments and torrents of scandals and wrong accusations to come her way, and then a refreshing south wind to blow upon that secret place that encloses her heart, her pain and her suffering hidden behind a mask called, 'Self'. A place she had gained control of while seeking for the happiness and pleasures she needed to fulfill her dreams and her heart's desires.

In this place where she had suffered resulted in a vast array of rejection and suffering and this she encountered while trusting totally in Him, not understanding that the reason He was allowing her to encounter these conditions was to bring her into His complete purpose for her life, which is to live and reign as 'sons' of God, Romans 8:14, 16-18 (KJV): declares that *"For as many as are led by the Spirit of God, they are the sons of God. The Spirit itself beareth witness with our spirit, that we are the children of God: And if children, then heirs; heirs of God, and joint-heirs with Christ; if so be that we suffer with him, that we may be also glorified together; For I reckon that the sufferings of this present time are not worthy to be compared with the glory which shall be revealed in us."*

The bride in her pursuit of happiness loses her ability to demonstrate by faith that which she could not see, feel or touch. She held on to and followed after that which was familiar to her senses, appeasing her natural desires of the flesh and not of the Spirit.

Through His divine intervention, He allows a fragrance of His love into her heart removing the mask and revealing a depth of expression that flowed as a river of living water from within her, exposing her innermost being, giving her a desire of becoming one with Him, and the ability of producing after His kind as she cried out!

Many within the body of Jesus Christ after going through the desired process of becoming *'heirs of God, and joint-heirs with Christ;'* should expect to also suffer as He did. Rachael in this story, during the nine months of gestation and delivery brought so much sorrow, that when she gave birth to Benjamin she named him "Ben Oni" son of my sorrow. She died never understanding that her (child) ministry would bring total glory to God.

Jacob named His son, "Benjamin, Son of my right hand" that which was familiar to him, a (Child) ministry he was capable of producing and promoting, one in which he functioned and was sure to be successfully administered. A (child) ministry that did not bring glory to God but glory to 'himself', he being labeled a trickster and a deceiver, passed on to his son an inheritance of his own personality.

During the latter years of Jacobs's life, his name now changes to Israel declared a word over Benjamin as he blesses him "*Benjamin is a ravenous wolf; in the morning he devours the prey, in the evening he divides the plunder*" *Genesis* 49:27 (NIV)

The Bride of Christ who is called in her hour to bring forth the power of the Almighty God, those who are only interested in obtaining status with their own selfish motives and desires will also in this hour labor to bring forth (A child) ministries after their own kind that will be called ravenous wolves.

Those who follow after the heart of God and seek an intimate relationship with Him, will bring forth (A child) ministry after His kind. Paul said in Romans 8:18-23, "*I consider that our present sufferings are not worth comparing with the glory that will be revealed in us. The creation waits in eager expectation for the sons of God to be revealed. For the creation was subjected to frustration, not by its own choice, but by the will of the one who subjected it, in hope that the creation itself will be liberated from its bondage to decay and brought into the glorious freedom of the children of God. We know that the whole creation has been groaning as in the pains of childbirth right up to the present time.*

Not only so, but we ourselves, who have the first fruits of the Spirit, groan inwardly as we wait eagerly for our adoption as sons, the redemption of our bodies." They will see in this hour the power of God in demonstration. The dead will be raised, the sick will be healed and the lame will walk again. The Bride of Christ will in this hour demonstrate the power of God in its fullness.

The Spiritual "Self" Identified

During the nigh seasons of my life, I had a dream, and in the dream I saw a vision of a woman who had moved into my mom's house after my father had gone to be with the Lord. I called it a vision because after I had awaken from sleep the Spirit of the Lord spoke giving me a clear interpretation of the type of a people as members of his body that were found in His house. In this vision, I had revisited my home after a few years of being absent and found this "woman of God" that I knew because of her popularity among the many churches where she ministered, but was not acquainted with personally she was now the occupant of our house.

In a conversation that she started, she told me about how often the Holy Spirit spoke to her, and how she would respond to Him in answer to every petition or every word of knowledge given to her. I listened for a while, as she gave me an exalted view of herself and her relationship with the Holy Spirit, declaring that she had been gifted according to the position she had received. She continued speaking as she shifted her body moving from one side of the doorway to the other giving me a clear view of her bedroom, inside I saw this young man lying with a sheet covering his body from the waist down, and the upper part of his body uncovered. After her conversation was over she noticed for a moment that I was staring at this scene with my face covered in confusion and suspicion, doubting that she had any sort of conversation with God in this condition she was caught in, 'sleeping with a man so young and she is calling herself a Christian?' I thought. Also after observing this picture my imagination began to run away with me, my suspicion set in and my silent uneasy expressions became obvious to her, I felt she was lying about her relationship with the Lord.

I began quickly to compose myself after she noticed my uncontrolled conduct, trying not to allude to anything as I listened to her continuing her conversation, sharing the many things the Lord had done for her and the miracles He continued to perform in her life. She immediately turned to this young man's direction, smiled and introduced him as her son. She appeared to be about forty years old and this young man looked about half her age.

She was a beautiful woman, who had just gotten out of her bed for the day with the most beautiful facial appearance, wearing an outfit that should have been worn in the daytime, a chiffon empire waistline dress in autumn colors, flowing down to her feet and on to the floor,

I had this dream between three and five o'clock in the morning, I got up, wrote it down about six o'clock, prayed for about another hour and the Spirit of the Lord spoke and said, and I quote:

> *"She represents today's type of Church and its members, taking over My house.*
>
> *A false church, operating sinfully, It is deceiving, beautiful to the eyes of men, but full of deception, Sleeping with her son does not necessarily mean that they are sleeping with their children, but hidden behind their persona is this* ***love of self, one's own flesh and blood more than loving Me, and obeying My ordinances and My commandments."***

The Spirit of the Lord speaks expressly today:

"I looked again, as I visited my house
She was not totally recognizable
She wore purple chiffon,
Draped over an autumn beige empire waistline dress,
The dress resembled a style that I recognized

INCEST

As Incest
That dress cleaved to her frame
Desiring only to be joined in close blood relations
And become one with her
Oneness with her flesh and its desires
Oneness, not with My Spirit,
Not one with Me
But one with her ***self***
A selfish representation of the flesh and its desires"

The Holy Spirit works through stages to sanctify us as He brings us into a closer relationship with God. The word of God declares: *"No man can come to me, except the Father which hath sent me draw him: and I will raise him up at the last day. It is written in the prophets,* ***'And they shall be all taught of God'****. Every man therefore that hath heard, and hath learned of the Father, cometh unto me." (KJV)* The Holy Spirit also draws us to the Lord our Lord and Saviour Jesus Christ bringing us into a position of having an intimate relationship with Him and as we begin to hear Him speak, with eagerness we wait in his presence to obey and follow each one of His commands as He communicates to us His purpose and plans for our lives. "*For by grace are ye saved through faith; and that not* *of yourselves: it is the gift of God: Not of works, lest any man should boast. For we are his workmanship, created in Christ Jesus unto good works, which God hath before ordained that we should walk in them" Eph 2:8-10 (KJV)*

When our Lord gave His life and shed His blood on the cross for us His shed blood created a new covenant with us and for us so that we could now be joined to Him becoming one with God. The word of God also declares in Romans 12:4-5 that, "*as in one body we have many members, but all the members have not the same office: So we, being many, are* ***one body in Christ,*** *and everyone member's one of another.*" So it is never about us alone, it is about the body of Christ as a whole.

As we become one with our Lord and Savior Jesus Christ, we go through a conflict with our new creation in Him against our flesh, but sufficient provision is made for our success through the precious Holy Spirit dwelling in us. Through obedience to the Word of God and the empowering of the Holy Spirit, we as believers are able to live a life of holiness according to the will of God as we become more and more like Him.

We do not see the real purpose for the anointing over our lives and what God has called us to do which is our true purpose in Him, until we're given the ability to actually bring to birth a word that has been spoken over our lives, and sometimes the lives of others within the body of Christ, nurturing and assisting them. "*Until we all come in to the unity of the faith and of the knowledge of the son of God unto a perfect man, into the measure of the stature of the fullness of Christ." (Ephesians 4:13)*

Through the Holy Spirit we have constant communion and communication with God. We have not just received the written instructions of God through the Holy Bible, but we are also able to receive instructions by hearing from the throne of God, directly from His heart into our heart. Holy Spirit also witnesses to us as

He declares from His word: *"This is the covenant that I will make with them after those days, says the LORD: I will put My laws into their hearts, and in their minds I will write them . . ." Heb 10:15-16 (K.J.V.)*

As God communicates with us, He speaks to our spirit the spoken word, be it a Rhema[2] or a Logos. [3]If believed and accepted it becomes a seed that is planted within the womb of our spirit. Fertilization occurs when this seed penetrates or is accepted within our spirit and the Holy Spirit of God unites or begins to move to bring the promise into fulfillment. But before this promise (child) ministry is brought forth, one has to go through a process of incubation, which includes three trimesters. Within these three trimesters, the body (Of Jesus Christ) goes through many changes, feelings of discomfort, body changes, pain and sufferings to bring forth an infant (Ministry) move of God, still needing to be nourished or fed with His word, growing up and becoming mature spiritual giants throughout the whole world, bringing Glory to God, **producing after its kind**, allowing God to again open their wombs, conceiving and bringing forth children, never remaining barren.

---

2 **Rhema definition Strong's.:** A word that God speaks to you directly, an utterance (individually, collectively or specially),; by implication, a matter or topic (especially of narration, command or dispute); with a negative naught whatever:--+ evil, + nothing, saying, word.

3 **Logos definition Strong's:** The Written Word Only, something said (including the thought); by implication, a topic (subject of discourse), also reasoning (the mental faculty) or motive; by extension, a computation; biblefacts.org

"May God himself,
The God of peace,
Sanctify you through and through.
May your whole Body,
Spirit and Soul
Be kept blameless
At the coming of our Lord Jesus Christ"
1 Thessalonians 5: 23(NIV)

Differentiating the process of God cleansing His Bride to bring them into an intimate place in Him, so that He can sow the seed of His word within them as they bring forth His purpose

The Story of Leah and Rachel, found in the book of Genesis, clearly depicts a description of a process that a man or woman of God has to go through to bring forth into this earth's atmosphere or give birth to the purpose or a move of God in their lives and or in the lives of others as a corporate entity. This process called sanctification is the manifestation of our character being changed into a character that is of Himself, washing us through the word, making us blameless, as He invites us into his bedchamber so that we may produce that which is His and of Him.

The Lord's pattern of love for His Bride is illustrated in Ephesians, as is the husband's pattern of love for his wife. The word of God declares: "*Husbands love your wives, just as Christ loved the Church, and gave himself up for her, to make her holy, cleansing her by the washing with water through the word, and to present her to himself as a radiant Church, without stain or wrinkle or any other blemish, but holy, and blameless, in this same way, husbands ought to love their wives as their own bodies". Ephesians 5:25*

There are times when different situations in our lives bring us to the place of questioning who we are as children of God. As the Spirit of the Lord ministered concerning His love for the church, His bride, He began to quote from His word the story about Jacob marrying Leah and then Rachel. He ministered that both Leah and Rachel represented a type of His Bride needing their physical body, their soul and spirit to come under subjection to His Spirit. He is Spirit and He can only be worshipped in the spirit. Both Leah and Rachel needed to be cleansed with washing of water by the word.

In a night vision I stood in the doorway of a bedroom and watched a woman of God making an attempt to take a bath, as her husband stood in the door way and began a conversation that sounded more like an argument. His verbal expressions intimidated her; he was accusing her of the possibility of having an affair with another man, something that never entered her mind. He was telling her she was no good and worthless, that he was sorry he had married her and because of her being in the situation he was accusing her of she was damaging his status in life. Mentally She was innocent so why was he doing this she thought.

It is a lie why would He not believe her. She was tortured by every word he uttered, It was like weight on her shoulders. Her heart was aching and she wondered why was God allowing this man to live as her cries soaked deep inside of her without shedding a drop of tear or showing any emotions. I stood there recognizing myself in her position, suffering the pain from criticism and rejection while going through the same experience as she did.

As I began to meditate, thinking about what I saw in this vision, the Spirit of the Lord ministered concerning Ephesians 5:25—relating to His Church. He ministered that husbands ought to love their wives as themselves, the words that are spoken to them depicts the true beauty of the expression. His bride must know that only He can wash them. Only He (Our Lord Jesus) can cleanse them and make them holy and blameless when presenting them unto His Father.

He ministered that the women of God have been looking to their husbands (Jacob—the world) to supply and provide the kind of love that only He could give, just like the Church looks to the world for the same. He gave His life for us (The Church) to make us holy, therefore only He can cleanse us, by washing us with water through the word. Presenting her as a radiant church without stain wrinkle or blemish but holy and blameless, with the same kind of love husbands should love their wives even as he loves himself, wanting her to become the best that she can be, bringing her into the purpose of God simply by the words that He speaks to her.

The Spirit of the Lord Ministers to His bride today:

"The words that I speak over your lives,
It will not return unto me void but it will accomplish My purpose
My will, creating you into what pleases Me.
I will hold myself to My word drawing you back to Me
Even if you go back into the world to fulfill your heart desires
I will draw you back to myself.
I love you"

Leah was not really loved, but she had the perfect qualities of a tender person. She was weak, her personality was easily misinterpreted, and her characteristics were easily identified. The word declares that she had a weak eye. Any situation that came about, she quickly yielded to. She married Jacob because it was customary that the oldest marry first, it was not about love, Jacob did not love her, he loved her sister Rachel and this was a problem that she was not in control of solving, or that she had made any decisions about. She knew that she was not accepted throughout her life as a beautiful individual or was ever described as a beautiful person, so she felt she had to settle for whatever was offered to her. She embraced the opportunity to marry Jacob as she grew weary of waiting, needing someone to fulfill her purpose in life.

She had a very low self-esteem, but she knew how to reach out to others in a concerned compassionate and caring way. She demonstrated that by doing all that she could to prove to her husband that she loved him. She wanted to make him happy enough to love her back, denying the emptiness she felt inside, that place that only God could fill, denying Him her total adoration and love.

Rachel's story is completely different from Leah's. Jacob, her husband loved her, he provided for her and she depended on him for her every need. Because of the improvement that she recognized in Leah's life after she sought her position in God, she could no longer identify herself as a person who was strong, independent, self sufficient, mature in wisdom and understanding. She began to doubt her ability in producing the qualities that made her flexible enough to control her situation; she turned to her husband Jacob and blamed him.

Until Leah and Rachel both found themselves in a relationship with the one and only true living God, their creator, the only one who could bring them into purpose, washing them through His spoken word, making them blameless and holy, they were unfulfilled, empty and barren. Creating other gods, (the world—their husbands).

As the Spirit of the Lord speaks to His people, He addresses three main functions of their spirit.

(1) **The conscience:** The sense of what is right and wrong that governs a person's thoughts and actions, urging him or her to do right rather than wrong.

(2) **Intuition:** Knowledge that comes by instinct or by direct attainment of the mind of oneself, without any explanation. We really "know" through our intuition, our mind merely helps us to "understand" the revelations of God and all the movements of the Holy Spirit.

(3) **Communion:** Direct expression and interpretation of the things shared between a man and God, a feeling of emotional or Spiritual closeness and fellowship with God.
Our worship of God and His communication with us are directly in the Spirit.

The Spirit of the Lord speaks expressly today:

"I have to bring a people away from their way of thinking,
An organized assembling of people,
Gathered togethe only to meet, praise and
worship me at certain occasions.

I require a people, who would be so absorbed in Me,
That they will allow Me to fight this battle
with the enemy through them,
In this place where the enemy is fought they have failed.
They have been resistant,
Not so much rebellious,
But they are putting up a resistance.

My people would not harken unto my voice.
The voice that they should have been accustomed to hearing by now,
They should know that I am not moving without the Church,
But within her
Because there are a people that I will use to do
a Kingdom work through, on earth.

I have called you into the Kingdom for this day, said the Lord.
I will pour out of my Spirit upon you, and will cause you
to do that which I have purposed for this hour.
Be obedient, I will lead you and give you instructions.
You will never be barren, you will continue to produce."

. . . . And this is where Leah and Rachel are introduced, representing the dedication of Gods people in obtaining the glorious riches of God in Christ Jesus our Lord.

And Labon had two daughters.
The name of he elder was Leah, and the
name of the younger was Rachel.
Leah was tender eyed:
but Rachel was beautiful and well favored
And Jacob loved Rachel . . .
Genesis 29: 16-18 (KJV)

And Labon said: "It must not be so done in our country, to give the younger before the firstborn. Fulfill her week, and we will give you this also . . ."

And Jacob did so, and fulfilled her week;
and he gave Rachel his daughter to wife also.
Genesis 29: 22-29 (KJV)

So Jacob married Leah and Rachel, Leah (who was the first to be offered in marriage, according to their customs, she being the oldest), and Rachel whom He loved.

Who have "I" become!

Have mercy on me, O God,
according to your unfailing love;
according to your great compassion
blot out my transgressions.
Wash away all my iniquity
and cleanse me from my sin.

"I" said I hated his ways when in reality "I" hated him
He had gone willingly against the thread
That thread of perfection that "I" have perceived to be the perfect family
One that is real for Jesus,
Don't rock this boat,
Ministry is eminent and no way are you going to mess this up.
I am going somewhere! How dare you mess up.
. . . . And I found myself in competition
Who's going to say the worst words to greatly offend who "I" really am?
Then and only then do I recognize who "I" really am,
Who "I" have become in trying to play god,
Creating what I needed to survive,
What "I" needed to come into ministry!

Lord Please forgive Me.

Leah

. . . . And Labon had two daughters: the name of the elder
was Leah, and the name of the younger was Rachel.
Leah was tender eyed; but Rachel was beautiful and well favoured.
And Jacob loved Rachel;
Genesis 29:16-18

☆ ☆ ☆

Leah had weak eyes, (Tender-eyed)
Her barrenness (Her emptiness—Her nakedness uncovered)

If one viewed Leah, one would not really see a person who had weak or tender eyes as some would say, according to the meaning of the word tender which is being delicate in substance; not hard or tough, someone who yielded to what she thought was pressure. She was easily broken, fragile in spirit, unable to endure hardship or rough treatment, soft hearted, sympathetic, compassionate, affectionate, and loving. She viewed everything, every situation narrowly. She never saw anything for what it really was, but always accepted it for how best it could please her. This is whom she had become, the characteristics developed hidden over the years.

All who looked inside and really knew who she was saw something else emanating from within her. No one saw her real beauty; they only saw her outward facial expression as a result of the pain she felt in the past, and in addition to that, the word of God declares that her husband Jacob did not love her.

> *"When the Lord **saw that Leah was not loved,** He opened her womb." Genesis 29:31*

Her womb was closed (she was barren), meaning; she was not able to demonstrate or express her inner-self. She was carrying all the attributes of a wonderful person but she was judged from the outside and not from the inside. God opened her womb shone a light of His truth in her heart and that light, the truth of what He saw her as, became a seed that she could not understand as she continued in a struggle with what had captivated her thoughts and emotions, she had become one with someone who did not really love her.

According to their custom in those days, as a religious tradition that had to be followed, the oldest son marries first; Jacob was a second child, but had stolen his Brother Esau's identity, his birthright, as he paraded himself as the eldest child of his father Isaac and mother Rebekah. As the eldest he earned the right to be married to the eldest child of his cousin Labon, Leah was the one next in line for marriage, so he married her.

The Holy Scriptures declared that Jacob did not love Leah. Knowing that and having to live with him caused an indescribable pain in her soul, her body ached to be touched, caressed and to feel the enjoyment of the pleasures that she felt the first time that he touched her, the night he made love to her and thought it was Rachael (The one he loved). It left such emptiness inside, the times when her physical body was close to him but distant emotionally.

In the relationship with his wife Jacob acknowledged his responsibility and felt obligated to perform his duty as a husband and she was almost satisfied, but because of his lack of communication in expressing his love, she knew he did not want to be with her he wanted to be with Rachel. Most of the words spoken between them were articulated in anger and silence, particularly the times when he would walk into the home that he had provided for her looked at her became very angry frowned his face and go off to bed.

She has been home all day lonely and in need of some conversation or just a 'How are you doing today?' A simple compliment would have been satisfactory. It did not concern him that maybe she felt the same way about the marriage. She had been pressured, tricked into marriage and really did not want to marry someone who did not love her, but she was making every effort to make it work.

He made her feel as if he was doing her a favor by marrying her and with that attitude emotionally she felt controlled by his behavior. He was satisfied with that which he could dominate and she was buying into that thought. She always made an extra effort to please him which was all the comfort he needed, he had performed his part and that was enough to give him a clear conscience concerning her accusations or disapproval of his behavior.

As she fell under the enemy's control, to her he was her worst enemy. She was married to someone who did not love her and that was made known to her every day even after having what she thought was passionate lovemaking which turned out to be done just as a good deed.

She saw herself in a condemned position because of all the bad treatment, the coldness, the uncaring and cruel ways she was experiencing, the negative words, which really did not bring out any good qualities that matched her personality, now she was beginning to see or believe all that was said to her and about her.

She lost all sense of purpose in her life, she felt her self-identity stripped and she only saw herself through his eyes. The things she would rather not think about, so early in her marriage tormented her. She ached inside, and she was troubled, grieved by what was going on in her home and she hated herself for being in a situation that she was not capable of changing or did not know how to change. As she mused over the thought daily of her being married to a man that she had no control of choosing, she felt paralyzed in a situation that was created for her and she did not know what to do about it.

She made every effort to prove that she could change the way he felt toward her by becoming more industrious, doing things that she thought he would recognize as significant, capturing or trying to captivate the meaningless attributes that many of the ladies of her time were using to please their men. She felt stuck in her marriage, the attitude demonstrated by the one she thought should love her was causing her too much pain. As she cried in prayer to her God, she believed that He would change Jacob for her, that He could make him love her and everything would be all right; this would create a safe loving environment for her to dwell in. She would become a whole and complete person, if only he would love her. But the Spirit of the Lord wanted her to recognize her own value. He wanted her to know that he saw her heart, and it was completely different from what her husband saw. He needed to share with her how he felt about her and how much he loved her.

He opened her womb.

And Leah conceived, and bare a son, and she called his name ***Reuben: for she said, Surely the LORD hath looked upon my affliction;*** *now therefore my husband will love me.*
Genesis 29:32

The Soul being ***sanctified*** *by the renewing of our minds*
(As the Bride of Christ)

"Listen to Me, O house of Jacob,
(The worldly desires and work of the flesh)
All you who remain of Israel, (the work of the spirit within us)
You whom I have upheld since you were conceived,
And have carried since your birth.

I am He; I am He who will sustain you. I have made you and I will Carry you; I will sustain you and I will rescue you."
Isaiah 46: 3-4 (NIV)

The soul of a man consists of the:

(1) Intellect; that place where we begin to understand, where we see our present condition in relationship to God.

(2) The emotions, that which we can feel and see, revealing our personality or self-consciousness.

For our souls to be sanctified our mind must be renewed to be the mind of God, our emotions must be touched and flooded with the love of God. Our will must be submissive and introduced to the resurrected Lord and we must love Him with all of our hearts.

We read in Romans 12:1-2, *"I beseech you therefore, brethren, by the mercies of God, that ye present your bodies a living sacrifice, holy, acceptable unto God, which is your reasonable service. (2) And be not conformed to this world: but be ye transformed by the renewing of your mind, that ye may prove what is that good, and acceptable and perfect will of God." (KJV)*

Our body needs to be presented to God as a sacrifice, and our mind needs to be renewed by the washing of water through the word so that we may be transformed into the likeness of God.

Our soul is transformed when our minds submit to the Spirit of God. After we are renewed in our mind we are automatically renewed in our emotions and in our will, for our mind changes our emotion and our will is influenced by our mind. If our mind is opened to the Lord, our emotion and our will must follow. Our thoughts, our will and our emotions become His when we have His mind.

We are not to be guided by our physical mind (our soul), which is our thoughts, our will, and our emotions; but we are to be guided by the **Holy Spirit** who communicates to us the thoughts of God, the will of God, and the emotions of God. God gives us the power to become spiritually minded through the Holy Spirit so that Christ's life can be manifested in us and through us.

This is where Leah now finds herself, in the process of finding the perfect will of God for her life.

God had revealed himself to Leah giving her an understanding of His great love for her, bringing her into a position where she could communicate with Him apprehend and worship Him for all that He has been doing in bringing her into a personal relationship with Himself.

Leah saw her condition, cried out to her God, accepted His words in faith as He began to wash and cleanse her with His word. The revelation that she had received of the Lord was placed within her and had become a seed. God needed to open her womb so that the seed He had sown could be watered by His word, take root and then grow.

The Spirit of the Lord continued ministering to Leah through the cleansing power of His word and in the continuing process of dealing with her mind, will and emotions, she had become arrogant; boasting in self, in her own self-centered way portraying: "I' am happy! The women will call me happy" But deep down inside was some degree of deception. Jacob loved her no more now than before. She had placed a covering over her heart, a mask that spoke silently saying:

> *"I will not allow myself to feel, I will not allow myself to be hurt again. I will not cry anymore to God because of the ridicule of Jacob. I have been hurt too many times expecting to be loved, looking for acceptance in a place where I cannot be accepted or loved the way I desire to be."*

Her associations became limited, as she often found herself alone, feeling ugly, hating and judging others because they did not see her for who she had become. She expected them to celebrate with her decision to follow Her Lord. The battle was not over, she found herself scrutinized by the people she loved and began to alienate herself from them sometimes feeling also separated from God. Her relationship with Him had grown, but her problems were still intact one situation after another and she just wanted everything to be all right, as she remembered a promise God had given her, echoing: *'I will never leave you or forsake you, I will be with you always'.*

Jesus understands and feels our pain, and He promised never to leave us. He says in *Matthew 28:20 NKJV: " . . . and lo, I am with you always, even to the end of the age."* Whatever we go through, He is with us. Sometimes He rescues us from situations; sometimes He gives us the grace to be able to go through the situation, but either way He is with us all the way.

"For the word of God is quick, and powerful,
and sharper than any two-edged sword,
piercing even to the dividing asunder of soul and spirit,
and of the joints and marrow,
and is a discerner of the thoughts and intents of the heart".
Hebrews 4:12 (KJV)

As the Spirit of God continued the process of the transforming Leah's mind by renewing it with His word, she began not only to hear of His opinion of her but now she was beginning to believe all that He was saying and what was formed in her mind because of what she heard she trusted His word as He ministered to her. She became pregnant with His words and was beginning to feel significant as He continued washing her of all that produced her barrenness.

He allowed her to see who she really was with the truth about her personality. She needed to know that she was worth more to him than she was to Jacob. She believed Him and as she began to trust Him she felt loved and knew that this was what she hungered for.

God's salvation is in the sanctification of our Spirit. He works through a continuing process through which we are gradually made holy for His use. Second Thessalonians 2:13 declares that: ". . . . *God hath from the beginning chosen you to salvation through sanctification of the Spirit and belief of the truth*". Holiness through sanctification also means that He separates us to Himself. Holiness is God's nature and He makes us holy by imparting Himself into us so that our whole being may be flooded and drenched with His holy nature and in presenting ourselves in holiness back to Him, we partake of His divine nature.

"Even as He chose us in Him before the
Foundation of the world to be holy and without
Blemish before Him in Love." Eph. 1:4 (ASV)

Jacob's blessings:

"Reuben, thou art my firstborn, my might, and the beginning of
my strength, the excellency of dignity, and the excellency of power:
Unstable as water, thou shalt not excel; because thou wentest up to
thy father's bed; then defiledst thou it: he went up to my couch."
Genesis 49:3-4 (KJV)

Leah's newfound relationship needed strengthening and on her knees through prayers she called out to her Lord all the more asking for Him to make Jacob love her for who she has become in Him. She felt important now, triumphant, anointed and gifted. Accepted by most Church members; at least they were aware that a change had taken place within her, something that was not acknowledged by Jacob.

She began now to feel unbalanced, disturbed that her new position drove Jacob further from her instead of toward her. She tried to incorporate her relationship with God and her purpose for living into her marriage, She had now gained a relationship with her God and in this, the fruits of the Spirit was evident: "*love, joy, peace, patience, kindness, goodness, faithfulness, gentleness and self-control, (Galatians 5:22-23 (NIV)* But Jacob could not identify who she had become, the true beauty or the work that was done in her soul. He could not see her exercising the ability to minister to others who listen attentively to her, wanting to know her suggested methods, solutions and approach in solving the very problems similar to her own. All she wanted to do was talk about her newfound relationship with her Lord knowing that Jacob did not love her the way that she desired; she was still looking for recognition and needed his acceptance.

As God continued sowing seeds of His love towards her, she pursued after Him with all of her heart. She listened carefully to every word He spoke to her, but more importantly was the fact that she could now hear and communicate with Him. Through the many long hours of communion with Him, she began to understand her purpose was more than just being loved, recognized and affirmed by Jacob. She began to see herself as someone important to God, she was coming into a relationship with someone who loved her back and who saw her for who she really was, not what she was thought to be, or spoken of by her husband.

As their relationship grew at prayer time God would tell her how much He loved her. He would tell her that she was a jewel, priceless. He gave her some gifts, the ability to hear him speak to her, now she could communicate her feelings. She had a newfound relationship with her God. He has become her lover now, her Father and Her Lord. She accepted His words as they began to wash her of all that produced her *suffering.* She had become pregnant with His affection, His love and His promises. The things that made her barren, her lack of love, low self-esteem and the things that afflicted her were no longer effective.

She had gained a position through crying out before God, He looked upon her affliction and that was most important. She had endured and stood her ground knowing that the Lord had not left her through it all. She was no longer afflicted by Jacob's judgments, but measured by God's affections.

*Leah **cried** out to the Lord; He **heard** her prayer.*

She conceived again in her pursuit of real love and acceptance, and when she gave birth to a son, she said, "*Because the Lord had heard that I am not loved, He gave me this one too.*" So she named him **Simeon.**

Jacob's blessing:

*"**Simeon** and **Levi** are brethren; instruments of cruelty are in their habitations. O my soul, come not thou into their secret; unto their assembly, mine honour, be not thou united: for in their anger they slew a man, and in their self-will they digged down a wall. Cursed be their anger, for it was fierce; and their wrath, for it was cruel: I will divide them in Jacob, and scatter them in Israel". Genesis 49:5-7 (KJV)*

Levi. *"Now this time will my husband be joined unto me, Because I have borne him three sons.*

The union between Jacob and Leah could clearly be described as two people who lived separate lives, having their own opinion concerning their belief in the power of Salvation and the fact that Jesus came and died for our sins. Most of their conversations were, what qualifies a person to be accepted or approved by Him, the end result being Jacob could not see himself in a position of not being in a relationship with His God and being accepted by him the way he was and Leah had found the depth of a truth that formed her intimate peace, comfort and intense love for her Lord. She constantly judged him by quoting the word of God, describing his evil actions and conducts toward her. She felt he only recognized her as a person who is being portrayed as a Christian using Christianity as a cover to hide the real truth about herself. An easy way out of not accepting his opinion of her that was constantly echoed in her hearing, after all, to him she was not beautiful, she was portrayed in his eyes as a woman who needed to be hidden away in the house because of the way she looked.

They were no longer one having or demonstrating the same principles. She lived now to please and walk in obedience to her Lord; as Jacob remained a part of the world and continued loving the pleasures that the world had to offer. She became frustrated at the thought of him comparing himself to her after she had accepted the Lord, had a relationship with Him, and he did not acknowledge having one, but he was constantly telling her that he was more loved by the Lord than she was, and that an indication of God's love toward him was in his blessings of the material things he had obtained, making her feel and relentlessly taunting her with words of how if she was definitely a child of God, a person who was not living in sin as he was not, maybe God would give her everything that she needed, and most of what he said sounded almost true, this was always a question in her communication with the Lord. Why was he being blessed and without relationship?

And in her crying out to Him in prayer, she asked Him to establish her in her independence of him, establishing her in her position as a woman of God, to be respected and loved. In reality there was not any indication that a change had accrued in his heart, she could not see the "fruits of the spirit" which would be the prerequisite of a person with whom the Lord had a relationship with, so she cried for the Lord to save him. She needed him to be able to understand the things of God that she was experiencing; it would have been more pleasurable for her to be able to share this with him as she thought. She felt that he could become a better husband to her if only he was "Christian" also, and thoughts like this bombarded her mind constantly as she tried to comfort herself, believing that one day God will begin to draw Jacob to Himself and he would know the truth that He needed a closer relationship. She wanted to come to some sort of closure in her life; she needed affirmation, but he was blinded by his own selfishness, his own self-seeking attributes, she simply wanted to be loved by him.

She took this to the Lord in prayer and as she cried out He began to minister, she listened attentively, allowing His words to continue cleansing her, He said:

"What happens, if this closure does not
include any of your desires at all?
The desire for the world to recognize who you have become,
What you're struggling with is the cares of this world,
Your desire for Jacob to notice that you're a
woman of God is a worldly desire.
You are still holding on, trying to become joined,
attach, or become one with Jacob,
Your fight is with establishing yourself for who you really are today.
You are fighting in an arena called, the cares of this world,
You're trying to attach yourself be joined with the cares of this world.
You feel as if your accomplishments or your position would
enable you to proclaim more of who you are in me
This position will not cause you to be more recognized,
Or would it prepare you for what I have purpose for you.

A man would bring a charge against you, despite who you have become.
You cannot allow the charge that comes to accuse you,
Demand that you close your mouth in proclaiming who I am to you.
Do not allow what has been said of you become you.
Do not be concerned or have any cares about making others
understand who you are in me or try proving yourself to anyone.
This position that you're in, do not look to the
world to confirm who you are in me.
Do not allow the ways you have been accepted by the world,
determine whether you are happy or sad, confused or elated.
Do not allow the accusations against you, or what has
been said of you by the world close your mouth. Your
position speaks for you; it can also silence you."

As God became more intimate with Leah He desired that she presented her body unto him and not to the world. He had been joined to her now and she began to operate in the gifts of the Spirit. He was her sustainer and her deliverer. At quiet times she would move her head to one side, wanting to just lean on a familiar place, the back of a couch or the edge of a table thinking how she wished it was Jacobs bosom, missing him so much but instead she felt something warm, and almost soft like it was him and thought: "No this feels like flesh, it can't be him, It was not Jacob, 'who was it." It was not Jacob, she was not tripping either, what she laid her head on felt like real flesh, Accepting the facts that it must be, she had just laid her head on the bosom of her Lord as she felt it, it was real but she could not say anything to anyone or even try to explain. This was Him and if only for a moment she felt whole, complete and totally loved, this she hungered and longed for from Jacob still.

Her Lord began to tell Her how much He honored her every time that she was faithful in doing His will as He continued to use her in the gifts of the Spirit encouraging, lifting others up when they feel despondent and giving them hope. She was happy now; she had been joined with the one she loved. Nothing in the world could replace Him.

She conceived this new revelation, this new understanding of how much He really loved her, and thought many days of how inconceivable it was for her to ever find such love. And the Spirit of the Lord began to minister:

"Once that cleansing is done on the inside of you by Me,
He (Jacob—the world) is drawn to that inside,
Where there is now love, joy, peace, gentleness and meekness
(The fruits of the Spirit as He dwells there),
Not seeing the outward appearance,
Which was hatred, variance, emptiness (or emulation),
Wrath, strife and heresies,
The Spirit of God that dwells on the inside then draws

his spirit to what is inside of you.
He has no other choice, but to love you and honor you,
because he is drawn to My Spirit inside of you,
Not to you unclean, but to you sanctified by me."

And she conceived again, and bears a son: and said, "Now this time will my husband be joined unto me, because I have borne him three sons", therefore was his name called ***Levi.***
Geneses 29:34

The goodwill . . . of God
"The King hath brought me into his chambers."
Songs of Solomon 1:4.

Judah. "This time *I will praise the Lord."*

Her eyes were open to the goodness of her God now, and she began to see that she no longer needed to be acknowledged by the Jacob as a woman of God. She knew her Lord recognized her now and even trusted her enough to send her out to do the work that he had purposed for her life, and she was pleased to do His will. The emotional disabilities that hindered her were no longer a threat, she had been joined with him which was His will for her life and she knew it from the core of her soul.

She brought forth another son, which was a result of her intimacy with her Lord, "*This time I will praise the Lord.*" So she named him **Judah.**

JUDAH, pronounced in Hebrew as "Yehudah," means, "Praise the Lord."

. . . She stopped having children.

We were created to have fellowship with God and to offer Him praises for all He has done for us, even when we cannot see with our natural eyes what he is doing, we should continue to offer Him praises. Hebrews 13:15 declares that: "*Through Jesus, therefore, let us continually offer to God a sacrifice of praise—the fruit of our lips that confess his name.*

He has given us a will to make up our own minds. His desire for us is to long to praise Him, to continually offer Him praise. Our desire as followers of Christ should naturally be to please Him. The most important role in the life of a believer is to worship the Lord in Spirit and in truth! Matthew 22:37, 38. Praise is not reliant upon our position or emotions.

"I will praise You, O Lord, with all my heart".
Psalm 34 9:1

"I will extol the Lord at all times;
His praise will always be on my lips" Psalm 34:1.

Our praises to God is not only required when things are going great and our prayers have been answered just like we want them to be, our praises should be continuous and real because of our faith in Him, Jesus our Lord, Jehovah Jireh—our Provider.

Because Thy loving kindness is better than life,
My lips shall praise Thee.
Thus will I bless Thee while I live,
I will lift up my hands in Thy name.
My soul shall be satisfied as with marrow and fatness;
And my mouth shall praise Thee with joyful lips:
When I remember Thee upon my bed,
And meditate on Thee in the night watches.
Because Thou hast been my help,
Therefore in the shadow of Thy wings will I rejoice.
Psalms 63:3-7 (KJV)

Jacob's blessing:

*"**Judah,** thou art he whom thy brethren shall praise: thy hand shall be in the neck of thine enemies; thy father's children shall bow down before thee. Judah is a lion's whelp: from the prey, my son, thou art gone up: he stooped down, he couched as a lion, and as an old lion; who shall rouse him up? The sceptre shall not depart from Judah, nor a lawgiver from between his feet, until Shiloh come; and unto him shall the gathering of the people be. Binding his foal unto the vine, and his ass's colt unto the choice vine; he washed his garments in wine, and his clothes in the blood of grapes: His eyes shall be red with wine, and his teeth white with milk."*

Genesis 49:8-12)

When Leah saw that she had left off bearing,
She took Zilpah her handmaid, and gave her to Jacob to wife.
And Zilpah, Leah's handmaid bore Jacob a son.
And Leah said, Fortunate!
And she called his name Gad. (Good luck, good destiny)
Genesis 30:9-11

Gad. *"A troop shall overcome him: but he shall overcome at the last."*
Genesis 49:19.

Leah's servant Zilpah bore Jacob a second son.
Then Leah said, "How happy I am! The women
will call me happy, so she named him Asher.
Geneses 30: 12-13

"Out of Asher his bread shall be fat, and he shall yield royal dainties."
Genesis 49:20.

Cleansing the residue

"There is a fire,
Can't you see the fire?
It's moving like a rushing wind
And it's burning everything in its way.
It's burning all the chaff,
Everything that is not God
It won't last very long
The fire of God is moving, and when it is finished,
You will see.
I am preparing a people to rule and reign in my Kingdom."

These are some of the important reasons for God allowing us to go through the Fire:

(1) **Fire will try our Hearts**

The fining pot is for silver, and the furnace for gold:
but the LORD trieth the hearts.
Proverbs 17:3 (KJV)

(2) **Fire will purge our character**

And I will turn my hand upon thee,
and purely purge away the dross, and take away all thy sins.
Isaiah 1:25 (KJV)

(3) **Fire will prepare us to become a chosen vessel**

"Behold, I have refined thee. But not with silver;
I have chosen thee in the furnace of affliction."
Isaiah 48:10 KJV

The Spirit of God began to work from the inside out. Leah's heart had to be tried, her character purged as He was preparing her as a chosen vessel. She had been joined to Him now with no distractions, nothing that prevented her from communicating with her God. Her spirit had been taken care of but now she needed to know how to separate the peace she was feeling within, from the chaos she felt as she craved that same peace within her soul. She found herself confused and in great perplexity as she watched her sister gaining favor from God without coming into any kind of relationship with Him.

The thoughts of Jacob continuing to love her sister Rachel at all was inconceivable and the thoughts of the indifference flooded her mind because she knew the price she had paid trying to please him, trying to make him see what a beautiful person she was. She had suffered more than her sister, she paid a price to be accepted even by her Lord, yet Rachel seems to just flow with blessings never needing to really change to have her sensual desires met, and all this troubled her. She felt constantly ridiculed by the negative words spoken about and to her in comparison to her sister Rachel. She thought that because of her relationship with the Lord, He would have defended her against such an onslaught and she became angry, and for a minute the thoughts flooded her mind that she had sinned against her God because of the way she was feeling, as it became more difficult telling others of her love for Him. To her this was the most painful experience that she ever had in her walk with Him. He was not speaking and she equated her natural feelings, not with the truth that He was really with her, but with a lie from the enemy that she was no longer worthy of His attention.

There were still some issues that she had not come to terms with. She had gained a position in her relationship with her Lord, but now she finds herself in competition, struggling with her sister in this fight for recognition even though her sister saw her beauty emanating from within, she continued to be critical of her own outward appearance.

She had come to a place in her God that she knew if she had a question He would answer it, nevertheless she confessed that in this season with Him, she had become angry, mainly because she felt that He (Her God) could lift her completely out of her trials and her struggles. If only Jacob could see her inner self and recognize her for whom she had become in her walk as a Christian. She felt no more a child of God than her sister who had not truly given her life totally to God.

Leah had become confused and felt tortured by this. Why would the Lord allow her to experience so much depth in Him and then suffer so much anguish? Why is there still resident within her the need to be recognize by others. In arrogance she thought that now she could compete with her sister, holding on to the fact that she had a relationship and Rachel did not.

She was above and not beneath, the head and not the tail. More confusing was that as she cried out to the Lord concerning her struggle. She felt as if He was not hearing her. God began to deal with her heart, taking off the mask that she had placed on to protect herself from people really knowing what was going on inside. Inside she felt angry with God, ever though she was being blessed and her situation was now changing, she was still noticing that her sister Rachel was shown just as much favor as was shown to her. She felt that she should have been treated differently, because she had a better relationship with Him than Rachel did, but instead of her communicating her thoughts, and sharing her struggles, she closed her mouth in anger, and began suffering the pain within.

She had become accustomed to hearing Him speak comforting words to her, sowing seeds of hope and continually bringing everything that He promised to pass and she missed His Presence more than His present, the precious gifts He had bestowed upon her. He ministered, but she could not really hear Him, Her thoughts covered her heart like a muzzle placed over her ear as He spoke gently to her.

God was removing, by His Spirit, all that captivated Leah's mind: her emotions, and the works of the flesh: pride, envy and hatred. Purifying her, while bringing her into an even closer communion with Him, He spoke as He began to minister to her:

"What do you do?
When you have made it through the wilderness,
The trials and tribulations that are assigned to give you
The characteristics of your Father God
When you have driven all the giants
The cares of the world—the pleasures of the flesh
That the enemy uses to keep you in bondage
You have walked around the walls seven times,
Blowing your trumpet until the walls came down
Completely breaking down the enemy's
stronghold—the enemy's defenses
When you have possessed your promises, what do you do?
You abide in Me, Your God.
You do not allow your possessions to become your god
Possessions meaning, the salvation of your family, the car,
House, big bank account or the ministry I have given you,
The gifts I have used through you

What do you do?
When you feel more comfortable in the fire,
After you have been tried, and already gone through the wilderness.
When you know that I am truly with you without a doubt,
Simply because you're surviving,
You're still alive.

What do you do?
Now that you have possessed your promises
Yet it seems that your relationship with Me has almost gone cold
You have grown up; your Father no longer holds your hands
But He trust that you will use that which
He has deposited in you as a guide.

What do you do?
When after you have possessed your promises,
You're still walking like an infant?
Who is just beginning to show off, first steps?
Crying, 'Guide me oh thou great Jehovah',
Not really trusting in His ability to guide you without asking.
After you have possessed your promises
And you're still empty, holding on to the cross of Jesus, His death
Not yet coming into the full accomplishments
and security of His resurrection"

That I may know Him in the power of his resurrection!

"Know this. That because of His resurrection, You have power in Me.
You are also seated in Power at the right hand side of the Father."

Zebulun *"God has endowed me with a good endowment; Now my husband will dwell with me, because I have borne him six sons."*

Jacob's blessing:

"Zebulun shall dwell at the haven of the sea; and he shall be for an haven of ships; and his border shall be unto Zidon."
Genesis 49:13. (KJV)

Issachar *"God has given me my wages,*
because I have given my maid to my husband."

Jacobs's blessings:

"Issachar is a strong ass couching down between two burdens: And he saw that rest was good and the land that it was pleasant; and bowed his shoulder to bear, and became a servant unto tribute."
Genesis 49:14-15 (KJV)

Now ***Reuben*** *went in the days of wheat harvest and found mandrakes in the field, and brought them to his mother Leah. Then Rachel said to Leah, "Please give me some of your son's mandrakes."*
But she said to her, "Is it a small matter that you have taken away my husband? Would you take away my son's mandrakes also?"
And Rachel said, "Therefore he will lie with you tonight for your son's mandrakes."
When Jacob came out of the field in the evening, Leah went out to meet him and said, "You must come in to me, for I have surely hired you with my son's mandrakes." And he lay with her that night. And God listened to Leah, and she conceived and bore Jacob a fifth son. Leah said, "God has given me my wages, because I have given my maid to my husband." So she called his name Issachar.
Then Leah conceived again and bore Jacob a sixth son.
And Leah said, "God has endowed me with a good endowment; now my husband will dwell with me, because I have borne him six sons." So she called his name ***Zebulun.***
Afterward she bore a daughter, and called her name ***Dinah.****"*
Genesis 30:14-21 (NIV)

Rachel

But Rachel was beautiful and well favored.
Genesis 29:17(NIV)

Rachel's jealousy—Her Insecurities

Rachel was just the opposite of her sister Leah. She was very beautiful on the outside, well loved by Jacob (the world) never needing to find within herself the requirements or characteristics that made Leah who she was. She had no reason to cry out to her Creator, nothing to complain about; she had everything that Jacob (the world) had to offer.

She was well favored, tough, never yielded to pressure and not easily broken; she never had to endure hardship or rough treatment, she became dependent on Jacob for everything and he provided her needs well. She was the one between the two of them, admired and loved by what one saw from the outside. (Pleasing to the eye) and not from what she possessed within.

"I counsel thee, to buy of me gold tried in the fire,
That thou mayest be rich;
And white raiment, that thou mayest be clothed,
And that the shame of thy nakedness does not appear;
And anoint thine eyes, with eye salve,
That thou mayest see."
Revelation 3:18 (KJV)

And when Rachel saw that she bare Jacob no children,
Rachel envied her sister; and said unto Jacob:
"Give me children, or else I die."
Genesis 30:1(NIV)

Rachel was aware of the advancement that her sister had made in her relationship with Jacob. She had noticed Leah was no longer disturbed about the marriage and her participation in what looked like a game that ended up as a trick not based on true love but based on a very painful insecure environment filled with resentment, rejection, and insecurity.

She watched as her sister began to bloom in a way that was hardly recognizable or comprehensible. Leah began to demonstrate and produce the characteristics of a woman much loved; by whom she could not tell. She only knew that she envied what she saw was far greater than that which Jacob (the world) was offering her. She was always loved more than her sister but now she sees her as an afflicted person becoming affectionate and even in her insecurities seeking purpose.

Jacob loved Rachel and she should have felt secured in that love but she became jealous of her sister, instead of reaching out to embrace her new identity in love, she became conceited with an over-exaggerated opinion of herself.

Her beauty stole Jacobs's heart and his love alone provided all the necessary essentials needed in boosting her ego. She became conceited and boastful knowing that she was favored over her sister as she thrived on others opinion of herself.

Her knowing that she was more beautiful and more important to Jacob than her sister Leah only exposed her self-centeredness and in anger she demanded that Jacob give her children, accusing him of being responsible for her inability to conceive. This was her cry for help—not really to her God but to Jacob. The fact that she could not recognize or take responsibility for the emptiness that she felt inside only proved that there was a lack in her ability to communicate with her God. She became jealous of the newfound characteristics she saw in her sister and she soon discovered that she was losing her self-identity in her admiration. Her beauty was no longer the vital signs that proved she was well loved; she needed nothing else to fulfill her cravings or to remain satisfied in a world that only saw her outward appearance but never recognizing her longing to fill that empty place in her heart, that place to which the Spirit of God was drawing her.

In her pursuit of her Creator she was afraid that the world (Jacob) would reject her. She loved him but she was no longer happy in their relationship so in desperation she sought to understand why she could not have what she so desired. She wanted to give Him children and he could not help her. This present condition questioned her existence and her emotions revealed her personality and her self-awareness That place where self-dominated was what God wanted to replace with His existence and His love.

"Jacob became angry with her and said;
"Am I in the place of God, who has kept you from having children?"
Geneses 30:2

. . . . And Jacob, her beloved husband became angry with her and said: "How dare you put that responsibility on me, blame your God.

He is responsible for the condition that you find yourself in." . . . And Rachel began to question Her God.

Jacob (The world) supplied everything that she needed. There wasn't a reason for her to seek any assistance or help from anyone. She had become so accustomed to him answering every request she desired that she had no need to cry out to God for herself. Her every cry was always supplied by Jacob. She knew of God from a child, but never needed to form a relationship with Him. She was never faced with any challenges, hardships or disappointments in her life. She was well loved and her only concern was how she might solve this problem of not being able to produce children.

She figured that Jacob either had an answer or that he was capable of solving it for her. But Jacob could not fix this one.

Then she said, "Here is Bilhah, my maidservant,
Sleep with her so that she can bare children
for me, and that through her,
I too can build a family."
Genesis 30:3. (KJV)

Bilhah, describes Rachel's independence, her lack of faith in her God.

In other words Rachel was saying "If I cannot have children let us find a surrogate, a substitute. Here is my maid Bilhah."

Jacob did not offer himself to intercede with her, asking his God to change her diagnosis but he agreed with her to try another method. He could not see or even fathom the thought that her behavior needed to change and only God could do that. He began to identify her as one who never took responsibility of her own actions or whatever situations she found herself in, who constantly accused him for her inability to achieve any success in her accomplishments so as another method of pleasing her, he agreed to the surrogate. Rachel felt satisfied more in her position, never wanting to recognize her emptiness, hiding herself behind a mask of **self-sufficiency**[4].

And Bilhah, conceived and bare Jacob a son,
And Rachel said, God hath judged me, and hath also heard my voice,
and hath given me a son, therefore called she his name Dan.
Genesis 30:5-6(K.J.V.)

Dan—God has vindicated me; he has listened to my plea.

Jacob's blessing:

"Dan shall judge his people, as one of the tribes of Israel. Dan shall be a serpent by the way, an adder in the path that biteth the horse heels, so that his rider shall fall backward."
(Genesis 49:16-17)

An exemplified characteristic of what is identified within the churches of today

She replaced her need to cry out to God for help, with her own ability to place in order the things that she so desired from Him, not understanding God's ability to grant her the desires of her heart. Incapacitating herself she only saw coming to pass that which she manipulated in a method that she controlled. Rachel needed only to be able to justify or support the fact that there were babies being born in her home and also the ability to bring forth the same joy that Leah was having was all she had planned to accomplish. She should have just taken the initiative and be happy for her sister but she could not because she longed to have what she saw in her sister as a result of her relationship with God. She did not know that at the time, but this was what she craved

---

4 **self-sufficiency**: Not needing things from others; able to provide what is needed, e.g. by making enough money or growing enough food, without having to borrow or buy from others

She exemplified that which looked like a god, deceiving herself in believing that she was capable of coming into her own purpose not in the purpose that God had ordained for her life.

In her view of herself as she began to rationalize, she began thinking:

(1) That God had already judged her in this. There was always another way out and she had found it.

(2) The work that God needed to do in her was not required because there was nothing really wrong. She was well loved and needed nothing else.

(3) This child is a proof to everyone that God also sees her position and answered her prayer.

"Rachel's servant Bilhah conceived again and bore Jacob a second son,
Then Rachel said: 'I have had great struggle
with my sister, and I have won'.
So she named him ***Naphtali****, 'great struggle."*
Genesis 30:7-8. (KJV)

Jacob's blessing:

"Naphtali is a hind let loose: he giveth goodly word."
Genesis 49:21.

A competition had just begun between these two sisters, the two types of Christians in Zion struggling within. As the Spirit of the Lord speaks:

"The Churches are being evaluated according
to the demonstrations performed,
Not according to a relationship that I desire to have with my people.
Instead of a people being produced, as a people who know and
love their God, you have produced a people who in essence,

are looking like that which I have designed;
That which I have purposed."

God had not opened her womb, allowing her to view herself for who she really was. She was deceived in thinking that she was just as blessed as Leah not needing to go through any of the things that caused Leah's afflictions.

To Jacob (the world) she was now equal with her sister; There were gifts manifested through her, not the gifts of the Spirit bearing its fruits of love, joy, peace, patience, kindness, goodness faithfulness, gentleness and self control, but the manifestation of the acts of a sinful nature, jealousy and envy.

The characteristics that she saw in Leah; the way she was no longer trying to please the Jacob (the world) allowing the world to gratify that place where she hungered; her loneliness, her anger, her insecurity and no longer needing validation from Jacob (the world) What brought her sister into prominence is what she desired as she became jealous of her. God opened her womb and exposed the thing that she had conceived as a gift from the world wrapped up in an ugly paper called fear. Fear of releasing herself from the world and the fear of losing Jacob as she began feeling insecure in their relationship.

And when jealousy is conceived, it gives birth to deception.

As the Spirit of the Lord began to speak:

"This is a reproduction of this type of religion today.
This has been reproduced within my people,
This type of religion that is not real
Not from the heart, a total deception.
Conceived inadvertently by the enemy,
They portray a religion that looks like Me,
but in reality has abandoned Me.

It has the power to totally deceive; it's conceited and has
the ability to look even real to a true child of God.
This type of religion has been examined by the best of my people,
It's like a bad apple, rotten to the core.
Outside it is beautiful and looks good to the eyes,
But inside, it is rotten, full of worms.

The type of church that I have designed for
my people has been abandoned
They all choose to go their own way,
Groups of people ministering all over the
outside of the perimeters I have set.
The umbrella that I have designed, no one wants to come under.
This umbrella with a people united for a common cause, to Glorify
and Worship Me in the Spirit, becoming one in the Spirit.

Until oneness is formed, they will always produce a deception.

Look at the churches of today,
very one of them in its own way, trying to
look more beautiful than the other.
Not in outward appearance, with materials put together by men's
hands, but by what demonstration of power is performed.
Who is loved more than the other, by Me supposedly.
It's a struggle to find out by searching,
Where my presence is more likely to be or not
There are also a group of my people who were being taught properly,
The manifestation of the gifts of the Holy Ghost
is mightily used, yet they think that they know my
judgments are harsh because of past experiences.
They would rather bow in secret.
They do not want to be seen by the false religions as being true to me.
They are afraid because in rebellion, which seems
normal, they will not be accepted.
But there is a remnant that will uphold my
word and keep my commandments.

Who will not bow to the slackness, this world demands.
Changing the word of God to suite their purposes,
Becoming content in their ***self contented***[5] *way of life,*
Self contented, self contained[6], ***self willed***[7]*."*

We know that we have come to know Him
if we obey his commands
But if anyone obeys his word,
God's love is truly made complete in him.
1 John 2:3 & 5(NIV)

The flesh desires the things of the world;
The Spirit desires the things of God.

"For as many as are led by the spirit of God, they are sons of God".
(Romans 8:14.)

Self in the church represents rebellion against authority; it represents pride, stubbornness, and lack of submission. The desire of self on the throne will lead you back to the world. The place where Rachel was left, struggling to detach herself.

God always leads us into humility and out of pride. Humility is a part of the process of dying to self. *Let this mind be in you which was also in Christ Jesus, who, being in the form of God, did not consider it robbery to be equal with God, but made Himself of no reputation, taking the form of a bondservant, and coming in the likeness of men. And being found in appearance as a man, He humbled Himself and*

---

5 Self - contented: Satisfied with what one has or with one's circumstances; easy in mind; not complaining, opposing or demanding more

6 self contained: Having everything required; possessing all the features and facilities required to function independently

7 Self - willed: Determination to have one's own way; willfulness

became obedient to the point of death, even the death of the cross. Phil 2:5-8 (NKJV)

Pride is sin and all sin causes a hardening of our heart toward God which causes us to become less sensitive to the Holy Spirit. Walking in humility and purity of heart causes us to hear God's voice more clearly and be more sensitive to the Holy Spirit.

He guides the humble in what is right and teaches them his way.
Psalms 25:9 (NIV)

As the Spirit of the Lord speaks to the Church today concerning some strategic fundamentals of combating the enemy of our soul, He spoke about our will.

"Any one that places themselves in front of
the enemy line without training,
Will become a casualty;
The training is design to prepare you, to break your own ***will.***
That you should become what you've never thought you could be,

Bringing you into My purpose.
The training is very hard and vigorous.
It is made to break you, so that when you go before the enemy,
You're familiar with the setting.
You move in with one thing in mind.
You only know one thing to do,
Not in your own will, it is broken
You move in doing the will of God.
Conquer. Destroy the enemy.
You win. You win, only if you destroy the enemy of your soul.
YOUR OWN WILL
A Child of God who gives up before this
training is over becomes a casualty."

Rachel was now beginning to get a revelation of who God was. He opened her womb as she began to recognize His love for her.

She was barren and desperately needed to conceive. She needed to experience the fullness of God's power. The stride she made in life without coming into a relationship with God was inconceivable, not comprehending the fact that God loved her as His own and wanted an intimate relationship with her so that she may know Him for herself. She was confident in her position; successfully acquiring all that life had to offer, never having to go through any trials or situations that were designed to bring her into the fullness of the reflection of God. (Not dead to flesh, but dead to the Spirit of the Living God dwelling within)

"Now Reuben went in the days of wheat harvest and found mandrakes in the field, and brought them to his mother Leah. Then Rachel said to Leah, "Please, give me some of your son's mandrakes." But she (Leah) said to her, "Is it a small matter that you have taken away my husband? Would you take away my son's mandrakes also?" And Rachel said, "Therefore he will lie with you tonight for your son's mandrakes." Genesis 30:14

The desire for the mandrakes was an indication that she had come to a realization that there were some things that she just could not do. Even though her womb was open which gave her the ability to cry out to her God, she did not, needing the impossible circumstances possible. She tried to attain by the only way she knew how. She reached out to something that was an alternative to God, sought after as a desire of the flesh something she thought would satisfy her hunger. (A mandrake plant is known to produce from it a love potion used to enhance fertility).

Rachel wanted the mandrake plant choosing to lust after the flesh to fill the emptiness she felt inside; once again reaching out to attain her own fulfillment in an artificial way. She needed that mandrake plant to fill her sensual appetite, to ignite her feelings (works of the flesh)

Filling again the place where God wanted to dwell in her with her own performances to achieve his purpose.

She was a Christian giving God thanks for something He had allowed by His grace and love for her but never coming into relationship with Him giving Him pre-eminence in her life. At least she was now beginning to have a taste of the truth of who Leah had become. This was the beginning of her cry for help not to Leah for the mandrake but a cry of her spirit—man to be drawn closer to her Lord. She released a silent prayer, opening a door to her heart as she expressed herself trying to understand why she could not remain in her place in the world and still obtain a position in her Lord. She considered herself a good person also, doing all that she thought was pleasing to God, giving and thinking of others, not recognizing that she thrived on other's opinion of herself so much that in her gratification she was exalting herself and not exalting God.

Making this trade with Leah for the mandrakes was in essence her saying that she needed to make another attempt to accomplish coming into her purpose without answering the call of the Spirit of God. She needed one more night with Jacob, one more night that could not fill the longing of her soul, one more night that would cause her to feel emotionally the pain of not being complete. That would take her back in a place of darkness and gloom, a place that would only bring her back to her knees causing her to cry out to God again for comfort and peace, bringing her into the place that God had ordained not expecting or planning to come into this place as she participated unknowingly. God saw her heart and answered her prayer. As he revealed Himself to her, that knowledge began to take her into the place required to bring her into position.

Then God remembered Rachel; he listened to
her and enabled her to conceive.
She became pregnant and gave birth to a son and said,
"God has taken away my disgrace."

She named him Joseph, and said, "May the
Lord add to me another son."
Genesis 30:22-24 (NIV)

(1) He remembered. He held her in His mind specifically for the purpose of bringing to Himself ultimate glory. He needed to show Himself as a light to the world, as a Savior, He used an impossible situation to bring forth a magnificent possibility making the impossible possible.

(2) Rachel did not need much faith for her desire to come to pass; because He gave her a revelation of Himself.

(3) He listened to her. He began to give her more of his attention as she cried out to Him for His help. It was her time to come into purpose so He fixed His ear in a position to hear her whenever she spoke.,

(4) He opened her womb. Allowing her the ability to release a declaration of her thoughts and the magnitude of her intentions from within her spirit, as she began to express just how she needed to cover herself with a mask of pretense, one that spoke clearly that she was a child of the Most High God. She was now His own and even though she knew Him she was now accepting the power of His ability to work in her life.

She became pregnant and gave birth to a son and said
"God has taken away my reproach".
And she called his name Joseph; and said;
the Lord shall add to me another son.
Geneses 30:23-24

Jacob's blessings:

"Joseph is a fruitful bough, even a fruitful bough by a well; whose branches run over the wall: The archers have sorely grieved him, and shot at him, and hated him: But his bow abode in strength, and the arms of his hands were made strong by the hands of the mighty God of Jacob; (from thence is the shepherd, the stone of Israel:) Even by the God of thy father, who shall help thee; and by the Almighty, who shall bless thee with blessings of heaven above, blessings of the deep that lieth under, blessings of the breasts, and of the womb: The blessings of thy father have prevailed above the blessings of my progenitors unto the utmost bound of the everlasting hills: they shall be on the head of Joseph, and on the crown of the head of him that was separate from his brethren." Genesis 49:22-26.)

The final move of God when it is born
Ben Oni
"Son of my Sorrow"

Rachel began to give birth and had great difficulty.
And as she was having great difficulty in
childbirth, the midwife said to her,
"Don't be afraid, for you have another son".
As she breathe her last, for she was dying,
she named her son ***Ben Oni—Son of my sorrow,***
But his father named him Benjamin
('Son of my right hand.')
Geneses 35:16-18

When Labon had gone to shear his sheep,
Rachel stole her father's household gods.
Geneses 31:19

The words that Jacob spoke to Rachel initially left her feeling hopeless and very insecure, as a reaction to her request for a child the words shattered her very being. As beautiful as she was it brought her to a place of dishonor and a misplaced identity, never being able to come into a perfect communion with her God as she spent most of her life proving her independence.

God had taken away her reproach and He had given her a manifested miracle removing that place where hopelessness dwelt and replacing it with faith in Him. Within the quietness of her own spirit Rachel sought to know the source of the power that brought about this miracle in her life. She had an encounter with God that left her with a desire to worship the One who was giving her these precious gifts, to come into a spiritual union with Him, but she still did not know Him in a personal way and could not reach out to a God that she did was not sure of. So she reached out to the only thing she knew well her father's household god. Just like her father, she knew how to work and control the system of the world to obtain whatever she needed. Through her communication with God she had not recognized that He was calling her to salvation, that her salvation was only the beginning of her calling. When she received His plan of salvation, He called her into, first, a closer relationship with Himself and then into ministry.

For by grace you have been saved through faith,
And that not of yourselves;
It is the gift of God, not of works, lest anyone should boast.
For we are His workmanship, created in
Christ Jesus for good works,
Which God prepared beforehand that we should walk in them.
(Eph 2:8-10)

God has designed a way for us to walk in doing good works, and it is by His communication that we receive through the Holy Spirit our directions and instructions to know where to walk and how to walk and so it was for Rachael.

Her newborn faith no matter how small it was, to believe that God would perform another miracle in her life was unthinkable, but she was called according to God's purpose which He had ordained for her to do.

Her faith did not go unchallenged; she had to hold on to that which she could not see, that which seemed impossible to her as if she had already obtained it. Something very difficult for her to do in a world where she was only recognized for who she was, "a beautiful, fulfilled and in charge woman of God" a mask that she had placed on herself only to cover her true identity deceiving others, but in reality deceiving herself, even after having her first-born she still remained the same controlling her own adverse situations

God began to cleanse her by washing her with the words that He spoke to her. He started by addressing her personal traits, the act of self-sufficiency and jealousy that brought her into a place of confrontation with Jacob (The world) the behavior that kept her from coming into communion with Him. As He dealt with her, exposing the truth of which she was, that pillar of hatred and un-forgiveness that she kept in her heart against Jacob began to break. Jacob saw her insecurities, her weakness and this angered her. All the un-forgiveness she held concerning others, for believing that it was her fault when noticing result of the vindication she sought against her sister when Dan was born and the great struggle she was having again with her sister in competition when Gad was born. She began to see the truth about her sinful nature as her life became meaningless and unfruitful. After all that she did to gain the trust and love from Jacob (The World) now exposed, everyone saw her as a failure and sorrow filled her heart, bringing her into a place of repentance and despondency as she began praying again that the Lord would open her barren womb and give her another child.

Godly sorrow brings repentance
That leads to salvation
And leaves no regret,
But worldly sorrow brings death,
See what this Godly sorrow has produced in you:
What earnestness,
What eagerness to clear yourselves,
What indignation, what alarm,
What longing, what concern,
What readiness to see justice done.
(2 Corinthians 7:10-11)

Rachel began to give birth and had great difficulty.
. . . . And as she was having great difficulty in childbirth,
the midwife said to her,
"Don't despair, for you have another son."
As she breathed her last—for she was
dying—she named her son Ben-Oni.
But his father named him Benjamin.
Genesis 35:16-1

In that time of her life when she sorrowed she brought fourth her second son conceived by faith: believing in something that she could not see. This was an unusual move of God that could not be predicted or recognized by the world. This son "Ben Oni—Son of my sorrow" was born while she was dying to the self that ruled and reigned successfully, bringing glory to God.

She died, not being able to recognize a great move of God that she had given birth to; she saw instead a representation of her condition at his birth and named him, "Son of My Sorrow."

"Benjamin is a ravenous wolf;
in the morning he devours the prey,
in the evening he divides the plunder."
Genesis 49:27 (NIV)

. . . . And as she was in her third trimester she found out that her child was coming feet first which was an indication that she would be having a very difficult birth, The prayers were being made continually to God for this power, but this method of delivery was so out of order that this child had to be turned around to a more normal position within her belly intensifying her pain and extent of the struggle of which she had to endure. The appropriate method of delivery is of course, Head first, the Body next and then its Feet, "**Total Divine order"** had to be brought back to the **Church**. As the Spirit of the Lord ministered:

"The pain and suffering that you felt in your flesh
Was an indication that there was a
Turning around of this child with in your own belly,
If this child had not been turned
To come forth normal, head first
***(Christ as head)** and not feet,*
The child would have burst forth,
Killing you, preventing this next move of my power,

Through the process of operating
Continually in her own ability
And not in my power—my mercy and my grace
*I had to use you **(The Intercessors)***
To turn this child around in her (The Church) belly,
Before she could bring it to birth

The Church has become powerless
In operating in that place where she was powerful,
They have used the manifestation of my power
To manipulate my people into fear,
Causing them to fear them instead of Me,
Indulging in greed and
Captivating the minds of my people,
Causing them to be deceived,
Operating not so much in her own strength,
But in that which she knew
The ability to operate in both Kingdoms,
The Kingdom of the God and the Kingdom of this world,
Leaning more to the worldly side,
Abandoning Me,
Yet acknowledging My Name in her work
I am God; there is no power in any other."

The moment had been intensified there were no signs of an escape from this great disorder, her body was tired of being weighted down, her feet were swollen, her face disfigured, and she could not stop herself from sleeping even during the daytime.

She (The Church) saw the show during the morning, the dawn of the new day—when God promised that He would make everything new. This show was the first indication that she was going into labor knowing that within the next few hours she would begin experiencing those labor pains that would make her back feel like it would split in two, informing her that a baby boy was on the way—a man child.

Her labor began within hours; her disfigured facial expressions became more noticeable as she cried out because of the most unbearable pains. Bearing down from within her belly, was a child pressing forcefully against the mouth of her womb, pushing its way through her birth canal as blood and water from her gushed forth like a fountain,

As the pain become unbearable, she saw her intercessors moving from side to side chanting, "Push" (in other words—pray more) as their prayers went up before the Lord for the manifestation of the power of God, the level of the anointing that would bring their ministry to a place of them becoming over-comers.

Over-comers with the ability to go into the enemy's camp, taking back all that had been taken captive against their will, moving in the power of God as an answer to the prayers of the saints. A people who have been given the anointing to move in power, taking down territorial spirits and demonic powers and bringing light into the kingdom of darkness. In this last hour of the Church, many will be praying for the manifestation of the power of God to be brought forth into this earth atmosphere today.

"I will pour out my Spirit on all people,
Your Sons and daughters will prophesy,"
Joel 2:28 (NIV)

In this hour of the Church, This new move of God—This new day, as declared by the Spirit of the Living God, the Ben-Oni's will be portrayed as an event that brought us much sorrow, but God calls them—Benjamin "Son of My (God's) Right Hand" offering us a completely different description from that which Rachel saw, proclaiming the truth of their purpose in Him. People of God used in this hour as God's right hand.

Rachel was later seen weeping for her children because this move of God was being invaded by the enemy to destroy the effectiveness of the purpose of God, and in the process many died, but His purpose prevailed as declared by John about Jesus: *"as many as received him, to them gave he power to become the* ***sons of God****, even to them that believe on his name: Which were born, not of blood, nor of the will of the flesh, nor of the will of man, but of God. And the Word was made flesh, and dwelt among us, (and we beheld his glory, the glory* *as of the only begotten of the Father,) full of grace and truth"* John 1: 12-14 (KJV).

Our Lord and Savior Jesus died for our sins arose from the grave on the third day and ascended into heaven and is sitting on the right hand of the Father forever making intercession for us.

Ephesians 2:6-7 (NIV) declares: "*And God raised us up with Christ and seated us with him in heavenly realms in Christ Jesus, in order that in the coming ages he might show the incomparable riches of his grace, expressed in his kindness to us in Christ Jesus.*"

As she breathes her last, for she was dying,
She named her son Ben Oni "Son of my sorrow,"
But his father (Jacob) named him Benjamin
"Son of my right hand"
(A trickster, a deceiver)
Genesis 35:18

PART TWO

Benjamin!
A Ravenous Wolf

In the morning he devours the prey,
in the evening he divides the plunder.
Geneses 49:27

Introduction

Rachel began to give birth and had great difficulty.
And as she was having great difficulty in
childbirth, the midwife said to her,
"Don't be afraid, for you have another son".
As she breathe her last, for she was dying,
she named her son Ben Oni—Son of my sorrow,
But his father named him Benjamin ("Son of my right hand.")
Geneses 35:16-18

Many in this hour of the Church of Jesus Christ will bring forth this new move of God in their ministries as a body or individually and because of the difficulties, through the process will die to the self that dominates. Many that are now embracing what is being prophesied to them will reject it at its birth calling the manifestation of their promise: "Son of my sorrow" because they will go through much sorrow to obtain it.

Jacob, who knew perfectly well that a child's name depicts his character, knew the importance of a child a name which determines who he/she shall be. Prophetically he changed his name to Benjamin "Son of my right hand" bringing glory not to God but to the flesh.

This child Benjamin's personality was similar to his father Jacob, the trickster, the deceiver and the thief who stole his brother's birthright . . . and even after Jacob's name was changed to Israel, representing the spiritual place that he had come to in God, operating in the Spirit and not that of the flesh, he declared a prophetic word over his son, acknowledging, that he was a reflection of who he was in the past, and not a mirrored image of who he had become.

As the child was being nourished by the Church, her breast was filling up with more milk than she could offer him in one feeding, so she found herself spilling milk (food—the word) mixed with blood from her breast into a bowl because the child was sucking too hard, or needed the truth of the word of God so desperately, not hearing sound doctrine but instead being filled with words that ministered to herself, becoming more '**self-satisfied**' and feeling '**Self-important**' having their ears itched by hearing whatever they wanted to hear.

The word of God declares in 2 Timothy 4:3-4: ***"For the time will come when they will not endure sound doctrine; but after their own lusts shall they heap to themselves teachers, having itching ears; and they shall turn away their ears from the truth, and shall be turned unto fables."***

What the Church has given birth to will surprise many. They would be surprise to find that they have delivered a ministry that came forth starving to be accepted, starving for real love. After the child had remained in that position for so long without the proper nourishment it's teeth grown out like fangs takes on the form of a ferocious looking wolf waiting to devour whomever crosses it's path, overriding anyone who they think are more anointed than they are competing with one another, never motivated to place themselves in any kind of order always thinking about themselves as the independent 'I', 'I am'.

While they were praying for one of the greatest level of the anointing that has ever taken place, one that will usher in the coming of our Lord and Savior Jesus Christ, in giving birth because of their self-centered, self-gratified and premeditated motives they brought forth ravenous wolves, preferring a counterfeit, being satisfied with Balaam's ministry.

"We have been prophesied to;
We accepted the promises of our Lord and have conceived,
And this is what we have brought forth?"
As the Spirit of the Lord ministered:

"Zion is in tumult, she travails, because she is in labor.
She must deliver, she must bring forth, and she must push,
You must travail with her,
Let her sit upon your knee.
She will bring forth, if you as a body assist her."
Says the Spirit of the Lord

". . . Yet no sooner as Zion is in labor
She gives birth to her children
Do I bring to the moment of birth?
And not give delivery says the Lord."

"Benjamin"
A Ravenous Wolf

In the morning he devours the prey,
In the evening he divides the plunder.
Genesis 49:27 Today's NIV

Watch out for false prophets

In identifying false Prophets that have come in among us, Jesus declared: "*Watch out for false prophets. They come to you in sheep's clothing, but inwardly they are ferocious wolves. By their fruit you will recognize them. Do people pick grapes from thorn bushes, or figs from thistles? Likewise every good tree bears good fruit, but a bad tree bears bad fruit. A good tree cannot bear bad fruit, and a bad tree cannot bear good fruit. Every tree that does not bear good fruit is cut down and thrown into the fire. Thus, by their fruit you will recognize them.*" Matthew 7:16-20 (NIV)

Twice He stressed that we will know false teachers by their fruits. Prophets who demonstrate "good fruit" would be lives that show forth the fruit of the Spirit "*love, joy, peace, patience, kindness, goodness, faithfulness, gentleness, and self-control.*" As declared in *Galatians 5:22, 23* There are two types of ravenous wolves that will come forth in this hour, dressed in sheep clothing that I will make an attempt to characterize. These ravenous wolves will feast on the emotions of wounded Christians, and those who are in desperate need of a 'word' will be ensnared.

(1) The false prophet who would gather just enough information about you and then repeat everything they have learned back to you. They will deceive the vulnerable Christian who goes around from prophet to prophet looking for a word. These Prophets prophesy out of their own imaginations adding their own predictions most of the times of your fall, promoting the enemy in all of his glory and demoting God in all of His power to save and deliver you from the very enemy of your souls) never edifying or building you up as the word of God declares.

(2) Then there is the subtle false Prophet who appear innocent, they come with their own motives only thinking of obtaining something for themselves, desiring only to appease their own fleshly desires, being guided by the spirit of divination, necromancy, familiar spirits that would give them just enough information to hook you, as when one goes fishing. These false prophets will pull you in capturing your mind, your will and your emotions. Totally debilitating your movements operating only in the flesh and not in the Spirit of God. Bringing you into death and not offering life and that life more abundantly as Jesus offers unto us.

The spirit of the Lord declares in 1Timothy 4:1. "*Now the Spirit speaketh expressly, that in the latter times some shall depart from faith, giving heed to seducing spirits and doctrines of devils.*"

A ravenous wolf is one who comes into the Church seeking to gain personal advantage. They are not there to serve or seek God but they are there to consume. Money and powers are the two major concerns that motivate their objective.

In the morning (when our night time is over, and we begin to look for hope again) we are devoured as a prey.

Paul warned in Acts 20:29: "*savage wolves will come in among you; not sparing the flock.*" We would like to believe that every prophet that comes into our places of worship are well intentioned, but the word of God declares that: "*Satan disguises himself as an angel of light and his servants also disguise themselves as servants of righteousness*" 2 Corinthians 11:14, 15. The word also declares in Acts 20:30, 31: "*from among your own selves men will arise, speaking perverse things, to draw away the disciples after them. Therefore be on the alert, and*, in Titus he wrote: "*there are many rebellious men, empty talkers and deceivers . . . who must be silenced because they are upsetting whole families, teaching things they should not teach for the sake of sordid gain.*" *(Titus 1:10-11)* Scriptures clearly warns us in Matthew 7:15-20 that there are many false prophets, and commands us to turn from them. Jesus himself tells us how to identify them.

(1) We will know them by their fruits. We are told to examine the life of the prophet and his followers. Jesus assures us that bad trees produce bad fruits and good trees produce good fruit.

(2) A good tree produces good fruit. Lives characterized by the nine-fold fruit of the Spirit listed in Galatians 5:22, 23: love, joy, peace, patience, kindness, goodness, faithfulness, gentleness and self-control.

*The **ravenous wolves** that the Church will accept!*

I remembered on this particular day during prayer time, as I communicated my heart's desire to see a move of the power of God in a massive way to save and deliver His people from whatever hindered us from coming into the fullness of His power. The Spirit of the Lord ministered for a while, and told me to 'expect a wolf', then He immediately showed me a vision, and in this vision I saw this beautiful furry white wolf in a sitting position, engulfed in the midst of this darkness, darker than any moonless night, pitched black. His head was huge with the most piercing red eyes, gentle and fearless looking. He sat there and just stared at me for about five seconds, and then the vision ended. I was stunned for about ten minutes after I saw that picture. I played that scene in my mind over and over again trying to figure out what it meant as the Spirit of the Lord began to minister:

"This is a type of ministry that will come forth in this hour of the Church, do not get involved. When a word is spoken over your life through this type of ministry, the consequence of that word could become detriment. There is no truth in what is spoken, so you're left empty without hope. 'from the sole of the foot even to the head, there is no soundness in it, but wounds and bruises and putrefying sores; they have not been closed or bound up, or soothed with ointment.' Isaiah 1: 6 NKJV. *This type of ministry is a set up before the real thing, a counterfeit before a great move but I will move to bring deliverance back to My people. Those who have been wounded, those who have been bruised by them will be healed and set free."*

Before the day was over I knew that what the Lord showed me in that vision had come to past. He was letting me know beforehand what I was about to experience.

My friend, Catherine brought this person by to introduce him to me at the place where I worked. Moments before she introduced us she pulled me aside gave me an idea of who he was and within seconds I was shaking hands with someone I did not know, but felt that somehow after his handshake and some comments he made he was someone I wanted to talk to. He said right away that he had already heard some things about me from the Lord and those words were what I wanted to hear, I was vulnerable and needed help, things were happening in my life that were just out of control and all I needed was someone or something to fix it.

Catherine introduced him as Bishop Ramon as she explained that he was visiting, holding meetings here on the Island, and it was important for him to meet her friends. She introduced him as a great prophet; he heard from the Lord, was highly anointed as she invited me to a night of meeting to celebrate his power in the gift of healing and deliverance. He held my hand after a very lengthy introduction repeated my name for a second time and said: "*We have only just met, and right now I am picking up something in my spirit about you.*" We sat down and for a while as he explained his gift to me and asked if I would come to his services because he had a word for me, I knew that I would have a good time as he invited me to come for just one night of a one week revival. "*I need to tell you what I see going on in your life right now,*" he said, smiling at me. Held my hand again and began telling me about a situation I was going through with my husband.

The things he spoke were 'on target' he was aware that he had gained my trust as he invited me into that secret place where I thought I needed so much to hear a confirmation of what the Lord was saying and with my hand still in his, he smiled, bowed his head and let my hand go. He had caught me. He ordered a soft drink and at the same time asked me if my husband was present, and I replied that He was, as I called him over to where we were seated and introduced him to Bishop Ramon. They spoke for awhile, sharing some light jokes about what part of the Country He was from. Making every effort to show my husband that he was leaving me with someone he can trust. After a short while my husband left us alone as the Bishop immediately turned back to me and continued a conversation with Catherine sitting right beside me as he disclosed some very personal information about me and the environment in which I live. As he spoke prophetically, he confirmed all that had been spoken into my life before by other prophets, confirming all my preconceived ideas of what must have been going on in my life which caused so much chaos, offering me answers to all of my suspicions. The things that I thought about seamed not so much fictional now but real, he saw my past he suggested that God had given him all the answers. He told me how deceptive my husband was and that there was a plan to destroy our marriage and with that information I felt for sure he had some answers as I began to confirm his accusations, explaining in detail offering him more information than he needed to know. He again invited me to one of his meetings so that he could break some chains that had me bound and that I should not hesitate for another day.

Before the time for the next evening service my friend Catherine called asking me to come by a hotel room to meet with the bishop explaining that he could not sleep at all that night before; that the Spirit of the Lord kept him up all night discussing my situation with him and He was also told to deal with me the next morning. He had to see me right away.

We met in this hotel room and after a conversation with him explaining his past and his encounter with demonic forces he recommended that I be anointed with oil, while he began praying. As he walked around a chair that he had asked me to sit in, repeatedly saying: *"I break these chains that have held you bound in the name of Jesus. Listen, hear them in the spirit, I break them off in the name of Jesus. You're going to hear a crackling sound, do you hear them? Sometimes you might feel like screaming. When a person is delivered, sometimes they scream. Let it out woman of God, let it out!"*

Chains that he suggested held me to some kind of sickness, a curse or something that someone had sent to totally destroy me. The symptoms he described in details were real, I was having them. I never heard the sound of the chains breaking, never felt like screaming. I was left disappointed because I was convinced I needed this 'deliverance' and nothing was happening,

He said that this was the beginning of a process that could only be finished if I began to sow into his ministry $500.00 which was a partial payment or the first of seven payments, covering all that I had in the bank in my name at the time. Just to say how accurate he was he quoted the exact amount I had on my bank account, He wanted it by the next day because he was leaving the Island in a few days and he had a lot more to do. He spoke declaring that God was ready to bless me and finally set me free but it was going to take my obedience to bring me into the full blessings of the Lord.

This prophetic Bishop was so clear and exact in his spiritual observation of me or in his ability in using the gift of knowledge, that I had a hard time not believing that he was not sent into my life by God to help me. But because of my prior warnings from the Lord I was a bit skeptical and a little watchful. The Lord continually reminded me about the wolf in sheep's clothing. If I was not given the word a few days before, I would not have recognized him, he was good. Even though I was pre-warned I believed for a moment that he was a true prophet of God and I could never get settled in my mind whether I should pay him this money or not, this was all that I had on my account. The Lord had just blessed me with this much after praying and asking Him for a bank account for more than ten years so I was hesitant about giving him the money. I asked him to do me a favor before I released the cash. I told him that because of this knowledge he had given me I wanted him to confront my husband about these truths. I asked if he was man enough to approach him with this information he could have the money so that I could be delivered from these symptoms. He agreed to my surprise saying that my husband was just a man he could talk to him. That he was not given a spirit of fear, and this is of God.

The next day he spoke to my husband while they both agreed that they needed some privacy and they wanted me to leave the room. At the end of their meeting I was told by my husband that the prophet confronted him and He told him to his face that he was a liar and that his accusations were wrong. He said that he gave him seventy dollars to help with a plane ticket, and he left.

This Bishop spent a few more days after he spoke to my husband and never got back to me concerning the money he had requested to bring complete deliverance in my life. The thoughts of my husband offering him seventy dollars or more than I had in the bank flooded my mind as I never heard the truth. I never got delivered by his prayers and never heard from him again. The truth that I do know after I thought about all this is that I remembered discussing most of these things he had 'confirmed' before hand with my friend Catherine. She even knew about the amount of money I had in the bank, dollars and cents. Did she disclose this information to him? I would never know because she never admitted that she did but this one thing I do know, the Spirit of the Lord spoke to me after this encounter and said that: "*I wanted to teach you, I wanted to show you how calculating, how brilliant, how subtle the enemy could be. I had to have you experience under one's (false prophet) control this act so that in the future you would be able to recognize this type of a ravenous wolf.*

I have anointed you. I have prepared you to be able to stand under this kind of attack; nothing will pierce your soul. He told you things that you knew to be true, everything you've spoken, everything that has been spoken to you, and even the things that you dared to think",

I was angry, thinking of how I had been deceived, I thought about how I knew I was to expect this wolf, but because of my long awaited desire to be free from what the enemy had planted in my mind I did not recognize him right away. There was nothing to prove that he operated as a ravenous wolf except for the word of knowledge from the Spirit of the Living God.

These false prophets after prophesying a thing that really tells the truths about persons but never solving or changing their situation, not offering any effective results are not unusual or abnormal in any way to the eyes of the beholder. If God does not open our eyes to recognize them and they being exposed, we would not be able to tell the difference between the true prophets or a false prophet. They speak the truth and we believe that they are from God, but we never see the manifestations of or the predictions declared determining the outcome. When a true Prophet of God speaks a word from the Lord we do see the manifestation, sometimes right away and sometimes we see the manifestation in the set time or season that God has ordained for it to come to pass.

Showtime

The Gentleman—Bishop—Apostle—Preacher—Prophet stood in front of the audience at the lower level of the raised stage spoke silently to a minister, as he pointed in the direction of a slim young lady with a pony tail that reached down to the middle of her back. The minister went over and escorted the young lady to where he was standing. He spoke softly and told her to raise her hands.

Removing his microphone from his lips to reveal in some secrecy a prophetic words that addressed her person as he began to prophesy to her, he asked the minister to pour more oil on his already drenched hands as he flicked his fingers in front of her face until her face was totally soaked, and then she fell backwards.

He motioned to two other people and prophesied leaving me totally amazed. This Prophet/Preacher/Man of God—who is worthy to be held in high esteem because he hears from the Lord—unpretentious, charismatic, engulfed in revelation and understanding of the word of God as he continued and I quote: "There is a woman here name Shannon", He waited for a few seconds and began to call out the name again: "Shannon will you come?" You're wearing a navy dress." He spoke slowly as if feeling for the right colors' to describe her attire." (No one moved) He repeated this a few more times, then someone came forth and he questioned her trying to confirm her name, however, she was not wearing a blue dress. But had the same name, "Is your name Shannon?" He asked. She replied "Yes", but as soon as she answered yes, another young woman came up wearing the blue attire, her name was also Shannon. The Preacher/ Prophet exclaimed; "Did you'll hear me say a navy blue dress?" as the whole audience begin to scream "Yeah, Yeah!" Clapping their hands and standing to their feel. He then drenched this young lady with oil and began to prophesy to her, and asked her who she was traveling with. "Is your husband here, are you married?" he asked, she answered "Yes I am, He is right there," as she pointed in the direction where he was standing. "Come up here with your wife". He said. And he came up and stood beside his wife. This prophet continued prophesying, revealing some things about her, the young woman gave the impression that she was quite surprised and shocked at what he was saying, so did her husband. I watched this scene unfold and I was totally surprised. The Prophet / Preacher, great "Man of God" had met these people before, but pretended that this was their first time meeting.

About nine thirty in the morning, I was sitting in a seat right next to this young woman and her husband, she was wearing the same blue dress as she was that night. Earlier, the Prophet/ Preacher entered the foyer of the Church and this young woman blurted: "Honey there is Pastor, see, Pastors weaving at us," she answered: "where?" Her husband asked, as she pointed to the door leading into the sanctuary and said: "there he is," and within the next ten minutes their Pastor walked over to where we were all sitting and greeted them both, he shocked the husband's hand and said to him "Hi, You made it, I am so glad that you could come" He replied "Well, we just needed a few minutes with you Pastor," and then he shock this young woman's hand and repeated, "I am so glad you can come too". He asked them both, how they were spending the day as they gave some detailed information of their schedule. They spoke ignoring the fact that I was present and then he turned towards me reached over and also shocked my hands and said "hello, I am glad that you could come, I replied, "How are you doing sir" I wanted to show him some honor, so I answered by addressing him as Sir. I was just happy to have met him, I did not idolize him as a highly recognized televangelist but I was always in 'awe' at the way he opened the word of God and expounded. This was "My man" and I shook hands with him—Oh my goodness.

I was totally astonished at this scene that night, I was a follower of his, and could never imagine him staging such an act, This was deception at its core and many believed and indicated their approval of him in their praises and thunderous claps, as onto the Lord.

Two nights before this conference started the Spirit of the Lord spoke to me and said:

"Do not look at the Church's Choir; do not look at
the speakers, the Ministers or at the Teachers that
are having a part to play in this Sanctuary
Look to Me He said, seek Me.
For the thing that I will do," says the Spirit of the Lord,
"Because of these meetings, many will be baffled.
Many are looking, expecting disasters, in this season, but in
*this season, **many will come to light out of obscurity and many***
will come forth out of obscurity, even as the light shines.
They will not see this; many will not see this,
because of what they are expecting.
Many will be deceived, expecting what they will never see.

Trust in Me and Live, Trust in Me".

The word of the LORD came to me:
"Mortal, prophesy against the prophets
of Israel who are prophesying;
Say to those who prophesy out of their own imagination:
"Hear the word of the LORD!"
Thus says the Lord God,
Alas for the senseless prophets who follow their own spirit,
And have seen nothing!
Therefore thus says the Lord God:
Because you have uttered (Spoken) falsehood
and envision (Imagined) lies,
I am against you, says the Lord God.
My hand will be against the prophets who see
false visions and utter lying divinations;
They shall not be in the council of my people,
Nor be enrolled in the register of the house of Israel,
Nor shall they enter the land of Israel;
and you shall know that I am the Lord God."
Ezekiel 13:1-9 KJV

False Prophets hearing from & communicating with God, yet walking in rebellion

Balaam in the book of Numbers was a Prophet recognized as a person who practiced divination[8] and sorcery[9]. In chapter 22:4-7 (NIV), he was summoned by Balak the son of Zippor who was king of the Moabite to curse the Israelites because they had outnumbered him. Balak made his complaint in verse 5-6, when he spoke and said: "*. . . . A people has come out of Egypt; they cover the face of the land and have settled next to me. Now come and put a curse on these people, because they are too powerful for me. Perhaps then I will be able to defeat them and drive them out of the country. For I know that those you bless are blessed, and those you curse are cursed. And the elders of Moab and the elders of Midian departed with the rewards of divination in their hand; and they came unto Balaam, and spake unto him the words of Balak." Numbers 22:4-8 (KJV).*

The elders who gave Balaam the message also took with them the fee that one would offer, just enough to pay for divination. In verses nine God came to Balaam and asked: "*Who are these men with you?*" and in verse twelve, "*Do not go with them. You must not put a curse on*

8 Divination: The art of obtaining secret knowledge, usually of the future, in a way other than genuine prophecy by the Spirit of God. The New Combined Bible Dictionary and Concordance

9 Sorcery: Magic, art of attaining objectives, acquiring knowledge, or performing works of wonder through supernatural or non-rational means.

those people, because they are blessed." Balaam obeyed. He could not go against God even if he was offered Balak's palace, and all the silver and gold—he obeyed when God told him to go in verse twenty: *"That night God came to Balaam and said, "Since these men have come to summon you, go with them, but do only what I tell you."*

More than once Balaam prayed to the Lord asking permission to go, trying to change the mind of God. He warned him to repeat only the words that he spoke but He knew that he would not obey Him and so in verse twenty-two God got very angry with him, ". . . *but God was very angry, when he went, and the angel of the Lord stood in the road to oppose him.* Why would the Lord tell him to go and to only speak what he said then got angry with him? Was it because He knew his heart and already knew that Balaam was going to curse and not bless His people?

In verse 31 ". . . *then **the Lord opened Balaam's eyes and he saw the angel of the Lord** standing in the road with his sword drawn."* In his state of disobedience he could not see in the spiritual realm the things of the Spirit of God. **God opened his eyes and he saw.** He **heard** the angel speak in verse 32: ". . . *I have come here to oppose you*". Then in conversation repenting, he answered in verse 35, "*And Balaam said unto the angel of the LORD, I have sinned; for I knew not that thou stoodest in the way against me: now therefore, if it displeases thee, I will get me back again.*" He confessed what was on his heart. He knew that he was not going to speak what the Lord had said after he had gotten there because in verse 35; the angel says again, repeating what the Lord had already declared: "*Go with the men, but speak only what I tell you, that you shall speak*". So Balaam went with the princes of Balak.

In the same chapter Numbers 22: 41 (KJV) "*And it came to pass on the morrow, that **Balak took Balaam, and brought him up into the high place of** <u>**baal**</u>, that thence he might see the utmost part of the people.*" Both were capable of going into the high place of Baal, a place where sacrifices were offered to other gods, a place familiar to them both. Balak wanted Balaam to see the situation from his perspective; he wanted to show him from the dark side how compelling the children of Israel would become if he did not curse them, bringing them under his control. This was the place where Balaam was capable of functioning while obeying his command.

In chapter 23:1-3 (TNIV): "*Balaam said, "Build me seven altars here, and prepare seven bulls and seven rams for me." (2) Balak did as Balaam said, and the two of them offered a bull and a ram on each altar. (3) Then Balaam said to Balak, "Stay here beside your offering while I go aside. Perhaps the LORD will come to meet with me. Whatever he reveals to me I will tell you. Then he went off to a barren height.*"

He separated himself from Balaak in this situation. He was demonstrating his worship, and adoration in obedience to God. The word of God declared that Balaam went off to a barren height. A place that had become barren in Balaam's walk with the lord, he was able to move back and forth in the spiritual realm and find that place where he met with his God in the past. Balaam was an anointed man of God, walking in the manifestation of the gifts that are without repentance, denying, unknowingly his God.

In the verse 4-5, God met with him, and placed a word in his mouth declaring a blessing upon His people and not a curse.

> *Now when Balaam saw that it pleased the LORD to bless Israel, he did not resort to divination as at other times, but turned his face toward the wilderness. When Balaam looked out and saw Israel encamped tribe by tribe, the Spirit of God came on him and he spoke his message: "The prophecy of Balaam son of Beor, the prophecy of one whose* ***eye sees clearly****, the prophecy of one who* ***hears the words of God, who sees a vision from the Almighty, who falls prostrate, and whose eyes are opened:***
> *Numbers 24:1-4 (N.I.V.)*

His prophecies included, blessing on Israel, judgment on Israel's enemies and an amazing prediction of the Messiah in Numbers 24:17-19.

In Numbers 31:15, Balaam advised the men of Israel, to indulge in sexual immorality with the Moabite women who invited them to make sacrifices to their gods.

Balaam was a false prophet sent to curse the Israelites; one whom God used in spite of his self-worth to bless them instead. This clearly shows the power of the Creator over that which he has created. The sovereignty of God in that He has the power to use whomever he chooses to do His will to bring glory to His Name . . . . "*For God's gifts and His call are irrevocable, [He never withdraws them when once they are given, and He does not change His mind about those to whom He gives His grace or to whom He sends His call." Romans 11:29 (*Amplified)

In Revelations 2:14; Balaam was again brought into remembrance. *"To the church in Perganum; Nevertheless, I have a few things against you:* ***"You have people who hold to the teaching of Balaam, who taught Balak to entice the Israelites to sin by eating food sacrificed to idols and by committing sexual immorality".***

Prophets in Rebellion

. . . Behold, to obey is better that sacrifices!
*For **Rebellion** is as a sin of witchcraft,*
And stubbornness is an iniquity and Idolatry.
1 Samuel 15:22-23

And when Rebellion is conceived,
Destructive witchcraft is what you give birth to.

A scriptural reference of a person who operated in the role of a prophet and later rebelled against God was found in the life of King Saul. The scripture declares in 1 Samuel 9:1-2 (KJV) *Now there was a man of Benjamin, whose name was Kish, the son of Abiel, the son of Zeror, the son of Bechorath, the son of Aphiah, a* ***Benjamite****, a mighty man of power.*

And he had a son, whose name was Saul, a choice young man, and a goodly: and there was not among the children of Israel a goodlier person than he: from his shoulders and upward he was higher than any of the people.

King Saul was a Benjamite born to a man of great power from the tribe of Benjamin. He was a good person, tall and just, fitting the description of one who should be chosen as a king, from his shoulders and upward, he was higher (Not really taller, but more arrogant) than any of his people, handsome and definitely the people's choice. (His name meant "Ask God")

In all this, there was never a mention of his relationship with the Lord, He was everything required by the Nation of Israel and God was giving them what they wanted. In this story, we will see how God moved to prepare Saul for his position as King, how at the onset he operated in the gift of prophecy communicated with the Lord, and later in disobedience, rebelled.

In the 10th chapter, verses 1-6, Samuel the Prophet/Seer anointed him with oil and told him to expect three things that would be manifested in his life to bring him into his purpose in God.

(1) Samuel 10:1-2 declares: "*Then Samuel took a flask of oil and poured it on his head, and kissed him and said: "Is it not because the LORD has anointed you commander over His inheritance? When you have departed from me today, you will find two men by Rachel's tomb in the territory of Benjamin at Zelzah; and they will say to you, 'The donkeys which you went to look for have been found. And now your father has ceased caring about the donkeys and is worrying about you, saying, and "What shall I do about my son?"*

Saul was told to expect to meet two men at **Rachel's tomb**, a place where Jacob 'sorrowed' for His wife Rachel. A place where Rachel was buried, after she prophetically declared her newborn son: "Son of my sorrow" The place where she could not recognize the move of God that she had brought forth, being a prototype, in this instance Saul had to visit this place in his life before coming into a place in his purpose. He had to be told that his anointing did not come about through any other means than sorrow; he had to know this. 10:4.

(2) "*Then you shall go on forward from there and come to the terebinth tree of Tabor. There three men going up to God at*

Bethel will meet you, one carrying three young goats, another carrying three loaves of bread, and another carrying a skin of wine.) And they will greet you and give you two loaves of bread, which you shall receive from their hands". He was to take two loaves of bread from these three men going up to God in Bethel. (Bread, most of the times representing the word of God. They will educate you in the word, enough to sustain you). 10:5

(3) "After *that you shall come to the hill of God where the Philistine garrison is. And it will happen, when you have come there to the city that you will meet a group of prophets coming down from the high place with a stringed instrument, a tambourine, a flute, and a harp before them; and they will be prophesying. Then the Spirit of the LORD will come upon you, and you will prophesy with them and be turned into another man".* At the Hill of God, Saul would meet a Company of Prophets, Prophesying. "***You shalt prophesy*** *with them and shalt be turned into another man*" (changing a prophetic word declared over Him by his father Jacob at the tomb of Rachel, his name was changed, from "Son of My sorrow" to Son of My right hand.

In Chapter 13: 9-13; King Saul began to disobey God and not keep His commandments. In arrogance he made a sacrifice unto the Lord which was done only by someone who held the office of a priest. He basically did what so-ever he wanted because of who he was.

In Chapter 15, He rebelled against God in his disobedience for the second time, and it became unto him as a sin of witchcraft, his stubbornness as iniquity and idolatry and God rejected him as King.

Saul continued serving as King even after His fall and continued to be successful in battle, operating now only in the flesh and not in the Spirit of God.

In Chapter 28, After Samuel had died and Saul was rejected as King God removed His Spirit from him. As a means of divine guidance he sought counsel through a woman who was still practicing necromancy; a person through whom the dead could communicate. He could no longer hear from God so he resorted to an evil way trying to operate in the Kingdom of God as a ravenous wolf after his own kind, 'Benjamin the Ravenous wolf, a deceiver'.

"Son of man,
Prophesy against the prophets of Israel who are now prophesying.
Say to those who prophesy out of their own imagination:
'Hear the word of the LORD!
. . . . Woe to the foolish prophets
Who follow their own spirit and have seen nothing!
Your prophets, O Israel, are like jakals among ruins.
You have not gone up to the breaks in the wall
To repair it for the house of Israel
So that it will stand firm in the battle on the day of the LORD.
Their visions are false and their divinations a lie.
They say, "The LORD declares," when the LORD has not sent them;
Yet they expect their words to be fulfilled.
Have you not seen false visions and uttered
lying divinations when you say,
"The LORD declares," though I have not spoken?
. . . . Because of your false words and lying visions,
I am against you, declares the Sovereign LORD.
My hand will be against the prophets who see false visions
and utter lying divinations.
They will not belong to the council of my people
Or be listed in the records of the house of Israel,
Nor will they enter the land of Israel.
Then you will know that I am the Sovereign LORD.
Ezekiel 13:2-8 (TNIV)

The wicket and perverse ways of a "Ravenous Wolf"

The negative effects of these ravenous wolves could be damaging to our psyche when we are given false hope as we believe it to be a word from the Lord. Most of the time we seek a word when we have been praying for a particular situation in our lives to be changed, we've labored in prayer for years and are not able to recognize that there is timing in the plan of God for our answers. Sometimes our prayers are literally held up as declared in the book of Daniel 10:12-13 (TNIV) . . . . "*Do not be afraid, Daniel. Since the first day that you set your mind to gain understanding and to humble yourself before your God, your words were heard, and I have come in response to them. (13) But the prince of the Persian kingdom resisted me twenty-one days. Then Michael, one of the chief princes, came to help me, because I was detained there with the king of Persia.*" A response to Daniel's prayer was held up for twenty one days.

There are times in our lives when we do not get an answer to our prayers in the time frame we expect it, we become anxious, especially if the answer is one that will cause us to hope again, one that is sought to build us up in our most holy faith.

When these situations that have come to try us have brought us into a place of reproach and we cannot offer up any praises unto the Lord we become silent, not crying out to the Lord in prayer because we feel disillusioned and empty. We begin to open our ears to anyone who speaks a word offering us some hope, which most of the times changes the course of our lives forever. If the truth is to be told we live to see the manifestation of the purpose of God for our lives. If we are given false information we are lead in the wrong direction without seeing a manifestation of what has been promised and eventually leaving us hopeless. If one is left in a position of hopelessness for a long time they will begin to doubt the true work of the Spirit of God in their lives and begin trusting in their own self-effectiveness, operating after the world system of lawlessness and not after the Spirit of God.

Even after we have been ravished by the false prophets of our time, know today that what God has purposed for our lives will come to pass. **There is hope, people of God.**

He has called us from our mother's womb to do his will, He declared to Jeremiah in the book of Jeremiah 1:4, (NIV): ". . . . *Before I formed you in the womb I knew you, before you were born I set you apart; I appointed you as a prophet to the nations.*" and in John 1:48, "*Nathanael said to Him, 'How do You know me?' Jesus answered and said to him, 'Before Philip called you, when you were under the fig tree, I saw you.*"

When Elijah ran in fear from Jezebel and was afraid that He was the only prophet left, The Lord spoke to him and said that He had saved unto Himself prophets who had not bowed to the rudiments of the world system, (Baal) but were kept to honor him, as declared in 1Kings 19:14. (NIV) ". . . . *I am the only one left, and now they are trying to kill me too.*" (18) ". . . *Yet I reserve seven thousand in Israel—all whose knees have not bowed down to Baal and all whose mouths have not kissed him.*" **There is hope!**

You will not come into this place of doubt.

This place of restlessness,
And you have not rested in a while.
The struggle within your Spirit,
This cry for deliverance of your soul is no uneasy feeling,
No unusual cry.
This is a Universal cry
The same cry that went out before I delivered my people out of Egypt.
In every circumstance or every occasion,
A cry like this went out before deliverance My people.

There is a stirring, a shaking going on within the Church.
A work that I am doing to bring order;
the order of things that you expect or that you see as order,
would be the five-fold ministry set in place.
My divine order is not only seeing this order of the five-fold ministry,
but also placing my anointing on the inside
to do the work that I have called them to do.
There must be a shaking, Uneasiness.
For there are those who are seeking notoriety,
Seeking My power without my anointing on the inside of them.
What you are feeling is the manifestation of my shaking,
Causing total uneasiness.
Think about the word that I have given to you before,
How that you would be like a tree driven by the wind,
Tossing back and forth,
But your roots will remain grounded?
You are feeling what is going on within the Body of Christ.
Think about it!
A tree, driven by the storm's wind being shaken violently,
What is left after the shaking?
If it has produced any fruit the fruit falls first,
Then the leaf, its covering, all the beauty of it dies.
Hope that the tree has roots deeply grounded or else it would topple over.
Pray that your roots are deeply grounded
Not only in my word but also in Me"
Say's the Spirit of the Lord!

A certain Levite in Judges Chapter nineteen was depicted as a very wealthy man. He had a concubine who left his home and went back to her father's house and sojourned. After a while the Levite decided to go after her with the intensions of bringing her back to his house because he loved her dearly.

Judges 19:1 (NKJV) . . . . and it came to pass in those days, when there was no king in Israel, that there was a certain Levite staying in the remote mountains of Ephraim. He took for himself a concubine from Bethlehem in Judah. (2) But his concubine played the harlot against him, and went away from him to her father's house at Bethlehem in Judah, and was there four whole months".

(A "concubine" was best characterized as a woman who is the lover of a wealthy married man but with a social status of a secondary form of wife who was often kept in a separate home. One who marries but is left no inheritance or dowry. It was customary in those days that a groom brings into a marriage some form of gift to present to his bride; a concubine had no inheritance of his).

(3)Then her husband arose and went after her, to speak kindly to her and bring her back, having his servant and a couple of donkeys with him. So she brought him into her father's house; and when the father of the young woman saw him, he was glad to meet him.

(4) Now his father-in-law, the young woman's father, detained him; and he stayed with him three days. So they ate and drank and lodged there".

The Levite in this story spent much of His time in eating and drinking enjoying all of the pleasures this world had to offer, never finding much time to pray or offer sacrifices to the Lord. The word of the Lord declares that this Levite spent five days with these arrangements before he moved on from a place of self-indulgence and comfort to an unsafe place and as a result he suffered tragedy, confusion and despondency.

(5)Then it came to pass on the fourth day that they arose early in the morning, and he stood to depart; but the young woman's father said to his son-in-law, "Refresh your heart with a morsel of bread, and afterward go your way." (6) So they sat down, and the two of them ate and drank together. Then the young woman's father said to the man, "Please be content to stay all night, and let your heart be merry." (7) And when the man stood to depart, his father-in-law urged him; so he lodged there again. (8) Then he arose early in the morning on the fifth day to depart, but the young woman's father said, "Please refresh your heart." So they delayed until afternoon; and both of them ate".

During the evening time of this concubine's life, the time when she should have been taught from the word and given enough knowledge to recognize her position as a lost child of God, she was found totally trusting the Levite's decision, believing his self-proclaimed knowledge and position in God was enough to protect her. As the nighttime drew nigh when she needed to be protected from the enemy of her soul, knowing that her safety was in his covering, it became evident that he sought protection for himself.

(9) And when the man stood to depart—he and his concubine and his servant—his father-in-law, the young woman's father, said to him, 'Look, the day is now drawing toward evening; please spend the night. See, the day is coming to an end; lodge here, that your heart may be merry. Tomorrow go your way early, so that you may get home."

In verses 14-21, after this Levite had passed through a City called Jebus—a place of strangers, where they dared not to stay for one night because they thought that the people of the City were too dangerous, he decided to stop in a place called Gibeah,

"And they passed by and went their way; and the sun went down on them near Gibeah, which belongs to Benjamin. They turned aside there to go in to lodge in Gibeah. And when he went in, he sat down

in the open square of the city, for no one would take them into his house to spend the night. 16 Just then an old man came in from his work in the field at evening, who also was from the mountains of Ephraim; he was staying in Gibeah, whereas the men of the place were Benjamites. And when he raised his eyes, he saw the traveler in the open square of the city; and the old man said, "Where are you going, and where do you come from?" So he said to him, 'We are passing from Bethlehem in Judah toward the remote mountains of Ephraim; I am from there. I went to Bethlehem in Judah; now I am going to the ***house of the LORD.*** *But there is no one who will take me into his house, although we have both straw and fodder for our donkeys, and bread and wine for myself, for your female servant, and for the young man who is with your servant; there is no lack of anything.' And the old man said, 'Peace be with you! However, let all your needs be my responsibility; only do not spend the night in the open square.' So he brought him into his house, and gave fodder to the donkeys. And they washed their feet, and ate and drank."*

Apparently while there, they could not find any place to spend the night, until an old man a fellow Ephramite from His own region took them in. *(22) "As they were enjoying themselves, suddenly certain men of the city, perverted men, surrounded the house and beat on the door. They spoke to the master of the house, the old man, saying, "Bring out the man who came to your house, that we may know him carnally!" (23) But the man, the master of the house, went out to them and said to them, "No, my brethren! I beg you, do not act so wickedly! Seeing this man has come into my house, do not commit this outrage. (24) Look, here is my virgin daughter and the Levite's concubine; let me bring them out now. Humble them, and do with them as you please; but to this man do not do such a vile thing!"*

The old man offers the Levite's concubine, along with his virgin daughter to the men of Belial, while they were in his protection. This is a classic example of what is being done within the churches of our day when a Preacher/Teacher or any 'Vessel of God' is found in a compromising position, operating in the flesh and not in the Spirit, in a way that is demeaning and one that degrades his/her character. The truth of the matter is, their flock are left exposed to the hungry wolves who are waiting to devour them as a pray.

(25) "But the men would not heed him. So the man took his concubine and brought her out to them. And they knew her and abused her all night until morning; and when the day began to break, they let her go. (26) Then the woman came as the day was dawning, and fell down at the door of the man's house where her master was, till it was light." And when they (the church) have gone through much trial, suffering and pain, they are left hopeless living with their minds snared, with no hope of escape from the thoughts of the words that was spoken in their ears, words which only blinded them from recognizing the truth of the love of God in their lives.

The latter end of a woman or man left in this condition is detrimental, yes. We are left, believing that we have been abandoned by the Spirit of the Living God when he should have been our shield and buckler in the times when the enemy attacked us. We are left believing that He was not faithful in supplying our every need when we have exhausted all possibilities of making our lives comfortable. Never finding ourselves in prayer and no longer trusting him or believing that He truly loves us. We are left believing that He is responsible for our downfall, and in essence we become angry with Him and we lose our joy and become despondent, **dying spiritually**, unknowingly but dying, Losing all hope. *(27) "When her master arose in the morning, and opened the doors of the house and went out to go his way, there was his concubine, fallen at the door of the house with her hands on the threshold."*

The Night is far approaching.
My children are scattered on the outside of
my covering, playing carelessly.
I feel an urgency to call them into My House,
before it gets dark.
When the night comes,
They will not see where they are going.
It's time to come In, My sons and my daughters.
Say's the Spirit of the Lord

Future Glory of the Church

There are a remnant people, a people that God is calling forth who are being prepared to accept this move of God who will recognize this child as "Ben Oni—**son of God's right hand.**" An **anointing** that will give the saints the power to go and seek out the real enemy of their souls, find and devour him in the morning, and in the evening they are going to divide the spoils (They are going to take back what the enemy has stolen, children, finances, families, and their health bringing us into complete wholeness, nothing missing and nothing broken.

In our time, the Lord is working with this remnant and is rising up over—comers to represent His interests in the earth, **a people who are in this world but not of this world.**

A biblical example of a remnant is a person or persons who fulfill the Lord's purpose for the whole body when the whole body either cannot or will not fulfill it. As an example, look at Noah. During a time when violence and sin filled the whole earth, here is one man who alone is righteous and pleasing to God. The Lord judges mankind with a flood, but does not make a full end, He spares Noah and his family and makes a new beginning with them.

Another good example is Elijah. He complained that since he was the only prophet left, he was better off dead, so he asked God to take his life. God replied, *"I have reserved for Myself seven thousand people who have not bowed down to Baal or kissed him (I Kings 19:18)"*.

And then Paul, better known as "Paul of Tarsus" as depicted in the book of The Acts. In verse 21:39 (KJV) he declared: "I *am a man which am a Jew of Tarsus, a city in Cilicia*", in the twenty second chapter, verse 3: he reiterated: "*I am verily a man which am a Jew, born in Tarsus, a city in Cilicia, yet brought up in this city at the feet of Gamaliel, and taught according to the perfect manner of the law of the fathers, and was zealous toward God, as ye all are this day.* And in Romans 11:1(KJV) "*I also am an Israelite, of the seed of Abraham, of the tribe of Benjamin.*"

His name was Saul, a man brought forth after his kind. A Benjamite "A ravenous wolf", persecuting Jesus and all that believed in Him, His Church. Later his name was changed to Paul (Ben-Oni—"Son of My sorrow"). As declared in Acts 9:16 (KJV) ". . . *I will show him, how many things* ***he must suffer for my name's sake***"). When God first called and converted him, the apostle Paul learned that a part of his service to Christ would be to suffer. Paul's sufferings were directly related to the great purpose of his calling. He was commissioned to go to the Gentiles in Acts 26:18 (KJV) ". . . . *To open their eyes and to turn them from darkness to light, and from the power of satan to God . . .*" (Acts 26:18)

His mission attracted intense opposition and persecution; "*Thrice was I beaten with rods, once was I stoned, thrice I suffered shipwreck, a night and a day I have been in the deep; In journeyings often, in perils of waters, in perils of robbers, in perils by mine own countrymen, in perils by the heathen, in perils in the city, in perils in the wilderness, in perils in the sea, in perils among false brethren; In weariness and painfulness, in watchings often, in hunger and thirst, in fastings often, in cold and nakedness. Beside those things that are without, that which cometh upon me daily, the care of all the churches.* 2 Corinthians 11:25-28 (KJV)

In the Book of Revelation *2:7, 11, 17 & 26 (KJV)*, the remnant people are called "Over-comers". The Lord addresses seven churches, and makes a special invitation to "he that overcomes". If we read through these messages we see clearly that the Lord is calling for a Remnant that overcame.

Ephesus

"To him that overcometh will I give to eat of the Tree Of Life, which is in the midst of The Paradise of God." Revelations 2:7

Smyrna

"He that overcometh shall not be hurt of the Second Death." Revelations 2:11

Pergamos

"To him that overcometh will I give to eat of the Hidden Manna, and will give him a White Stone, and in the Stone a new name written, which no man knoweth saving he that receiveth it." Revelations 2:17

Thyatira

(26) "And he that overcometh, and keepeth My works unto the end, to him will I give power over the nation. (27) And he shall rule them with a rod of iron; as the vessels of a potter shall they be broken to shivers: even as I received of my Father. (28) And I will give him the morning star". Revelations 2:26-28

In Revelations the third chapter: Sardis

(5) He that overcometh, the same shall be clothed in white raiment; and I will not blot out his name out of the book of life, but I will confess his name before my Father, and before his angels.

Philadelphia

> *(12) Him that overcometh will I make a pillar in the temple of my God, and he shall go no more out: and I will write upon him the name of my God, and the name of the city of my God, which is new Jerusalem, which cometh down out of heaven from my God: and I will write upon him my new name.*

Laodiceans

> *(21) To him that overcometh will I grant to sit with me in my throne, even as I also overcame, and am set down with my Father in his throne.*

The Ben Oni's (Son of my sorrow) would be easily identified with that which has held them captives in the past; and will be able to go into the enemy's camp and find a door through recognition, open it and set the captives free. Those captivated by the enemy in their minds, ushering in also the kingdom of God into the earth, taking total dominion.

This last move of God is the strength of the church; the ministry and manifestation of the anointing that will make the church glorious, without spot or blemish, bringing the church to perfection, bringing forth the manifestation of the **sons of God.**

> *The creation waits in eager expectation for the* ***sons of God*** *to be revealed. For the creation was subjected to frustration, not by its own choice, but by the will of the one who subjected it, in hope, that the creation itself will be liberated from its bondage to decay and brought into the glorious freedom of the children of God.*

> *We know that the whole creation has been groaning as in the pains of childbirth right up to the present time. Not only so, but we ourselves, who have the first fruits of the Spirit, groan inwardly as we wait eagerly for our adoption as sons, the redemption of our bodies. For in*

this hope we were saved. But hope that is seen is no hope at all. Who hopes for what he already has? But if we hope for what we do not yet have, we wait for it patiently.
Romans 8:19-25 (NIV)

As the Spiritual Church (Israel) continues to be birthed out of the carnal Church (Jacob, as he operated in the flesh), we will begin to see the sons of God manifested, men and women who have died to self and who are about walking in obedience to the will of their Father God and in His purpose for their lives. Men and women who seek the wisdom of God in making decisions, who know for sure and are very familiar with the scripture that declares *"for in him we live and move and have our being"* Acts 17:28 (on a more personal note) "In Him I live, in Him I move and only in Him I am." because they know that without him they cannot do anything.

Men and women who are led by the Spirit of the living God, who know their Father and obey Him in humility, understanding that it is all about Him and not about who we have become in Him, Glorifying God and not ourselves, representing Him and not the "self" that dominates.

"This is a time for the church to give birth to the Holy Spirit.

During the birth of our Lord and Savior Jesus Christ, there was much sorrow, the rulers and leaders of that time—King Herod sought to kill him even as an infant child. So in this hour, the church of the Lord Jesus Christ, the bride of Christ is bringing forth the power of God in it's fullness through the person of the Holy Ghost, They will go through much struggle, much pain during the period of delivery. Much will happen that will cause you to cry out, and you will become weary even in your crying out, but do not give up, persevere, persevere, loose all that entraps you, all that entangles. Persevere, persevere".

The Spirit of the Lord spoke in this season of His timing

There is Hope for the Hopeless, people of God!

For as many as are led by the Spirit of God,
They are the sons of God.
Romans 8:14 KJV

At the onset of the ministry one begins to operated in the gifts that accompanies the calling of God on their lives, for example: as a prophet, you begin to speak what it is that the Lord would have you to say and it is most of the time accepted by the believer and is manifested in its due season. The prophet or prophetess operates in the gift successfully for a while and then somehow out of nowhere it seems some adverse difficulty occurs. The loss of a close family member that you have prayed for to be healed, or sudden disaster that strikes, leaving you breathless and wanting to just give up and die. You've lost your job and have no neans of supporting your family or whatever caught you off guard has now become an unbearable situation. Most of the time the end results of going through theses adversities causes nothing else but pain and suffering, leaving you with questions that just cannot be answered, wondering: "Are these troubles because of some wrong things I did in the past. Are there any curses attached to my family lineage that has been passed down to me, and now I am cursed. Did I offend anyone or maybe I have not forgiven anyone in the past?" As we begin to blame ourselves for the condition we find ourselves in.

The Spirit of the Lord ministered that in this hour, even after we have been ministered to by the prophets, and have given birth to various ministries, watching them thrive for a while in its infant stages and even through adolescence; many have given up because of the various <u>adversities</u> that have came to try us. We are left bewildered and are no longer understanding our position or calling in His Kingdom. He declares that He is going to raise us up to be able to recognize that in His Sovereignty He has brought total glory to His name, bringing us into His purpose for our lives. In this, He is also raising us up to recognize the place where we have stopped trusting Him, where we have allowed our calling and ministries to die. With this knowledge, He wants to bring us to the place of not only declaring our position in Him, but also walking and demonstrating His power among the Nations, declaring that "the Kingdom of God has come." People of God, preachers, teachers, apostles and evangelist; begin to breathe life back into the lives of those who have lost hope. He has given us in detail, three examples, where a prophetic word was given, accepted as a seed, given birth to and in the process of time all hope was lost because the word that they saw came to pass, died before it had been nurtured or matured. 1 Kings 17:8-24, 2 Kings 4:8-17 and Luke 8:49, 55.

(1) The Widow at Zarephath, 1King 17:14, 16, 17-24:

> **The prophecy:** "*For thus saith the LORD God of Israel, The barrel of meal shall not waste, neither shall the cruse of oil fail, until the day that the LORD sendeth rain upon the earth.*
>
> ***(16) And the barrel of meal wasted not, neither did the cruse of oil fail, according to the word of the LORD, which he spake by Elijah.***
>
> *(17) And it came to pass after these things that the son of the woman, the mistress of the house, fell sick; and his sickness was so sore, that there was no breath left in him. (18) And she*

said unto Elijah, What have I to do with thee, O thou man of God? Art thou come unto me to call my sin to remembrance, and to slay my son? (19) And he said unto her, Give me thy son. And he took him out of her bosom, and carried him up into a loft, where he abode, and laid him upon his own bed. (She saw a great move of God, a miracle, but yet she saw her son died.)

(20) And he cried unto the LORD, and said, O LORD my God, hast thou also brought evil upon the widow with whom I sojourn, by slaying her son? (21) And he stretched himself upon the child three times, and cried unto the LORD, and said, ***O LORD my God, I pray thee, let this child's soul come into him again. (Soul—mind, will and emotions).***

(22) And the LORD heard the voice of Elijah; and the soul of the child came into him again, and he revived. (23) And Elijah took the child, and brought him down out of the chamber into the house, and delivered him unto his mother: and Elijah said, See, thy son liveth. (24) And the woman said to Elijah, now by this I know that thou art a man of God, and that ***the word of the LORD in thy mouth is truth.***

(2) ***The Shunammite Woman***

2 Kings 4:18-37: (Elisha—probably seeing his predecessor, Elijah performing a miracle like the one he was about to perform, and having received his mantle in double proportion followed his directions and the child lived also in this next story).

The Prophecy . . . . "At this season next year you will embrace a son" *`And she said, "No, my lord, O man of God, do not lie to your maidservant."* ***(17) The woman conceived and bore a son at that season the next year, as Elisha had said to her.***

(18) When the child was grown, the day came that he went out to his father to the reapers. (19) He said to his father, "My head, my head." And he said to his servant, "Carry him to his mother." (20) When he had taken him and brought him to his mother, <u>he sat on her lap until noon, and then died.</u>

(32) When Elisha came into the house, behold the lad was dead and laid on his bed. (33) So, he entered and shut the door behind them both and prayed to the Lord. ***(34) And he went up and lay on the child, and put his mouth on his mouth and his eyes on his eyes and his hands on his hands, and he stretched himself on him;*** *and the flesh of the child became warm. (35) Then he returned and walked in the house once back and forth, and went up and stretched himself on him; and the lad sneezed seven times and the lad opened his eyes. (36) He called Gehazi and said, "Call this Shunammite." So he called her. And when she came in to him, he said, "Take up your son." (37) Then she went in and fell at his feet and bowed herself to the ground, and she took up her son and went out.*

(3) The Spirit of the Lord would have His prophets to know in this hour that, the works that He did, we will do greater. In this example of Him raising a child in St. Luke 8:49-56, He simply spoke to her spirit and said "Maid Arise" and her spirit came again to her (The Prophecy **John 14:12:** "*Verily, verily, I say unto you, He that believeth on me, the* ***works*** *that I do shall he do also; and* ***greater works*** *than these shall he do; because I go unto my Father*") . . . . *(49) While he yet spake, there cometh one from the ruler of the synagogue's house, saying to him, Thy daughter is dead; trouble not the Master. (50) But when Jesus heard it, he answered him, saying, Fear not: believe only, and she shall be made whole. (51) And when he came into the house, he suffered no man to go in, save Peter, and James, and John, and the father and the mother of the maiden. (52) And all wept, and bewailed*

*her: but he said, Weep not; she is not dead, but sleepeth. (53) And they laughed him to scorn, knowing that she was dead. (54) And he put them all out, and took her by the hand, and called, saying, Maid, (what ever your ministry or the prophetic word given that caused your ministry to flourish and then died), **arise**. (55) And her **spirit** came again, and she arose straightway: and he commanded to give her meat. (56) And her parents were astonished: but he charged them that they should tell no man what was done.*

* * *

The Spirit of the Lord ministers today People of God:

(1) *"Take the child 'that ministry which has died' into your chamber, that place where you meet with me, where my seed can be deposited.*

(2) *Place your mouth on their mouths, Speak to them declaring their destiny, declaring My goodness in the past and pointing them to their most needed position in My Kingdom.*

(3) *Place your eyes on their eyes, not literally, but begin to show them what it is that I am allowing you to see, the things that have hindered them from advancing, seeing and presenting again the whole man positioned in Me, aligning him/her, bringing them again into alignment with My promises for their lives, knowing that My word will not return to Me void but it will accomplish what I have sent it to do.*

(4) *And place your hands on their hands, giving them back the ministry that I have assigned to them, the power of authority to operate in my Kingdom, picking them up by the hand and saying to them, in the name of Jesus "Arise, come forth, take your position."*

As we give birth
"To the exceeding greatness of God's power"
Manifested through the Holy Spirit

We know that the whole creation has been groaning as in the pains of childbirth right up to the present time. Not only so, but we ourselves, who have the first fruits of the Spirit, groan inwardly as we wait eagerly for our adoption as sons,
The redemption of our bodies.
For in this hope we were saved. But hope that is seen is no hope at all. Who hopes for what he already has? But if we hope for what we do not yet have, we wait for it patiently.
Romans 8:22-25

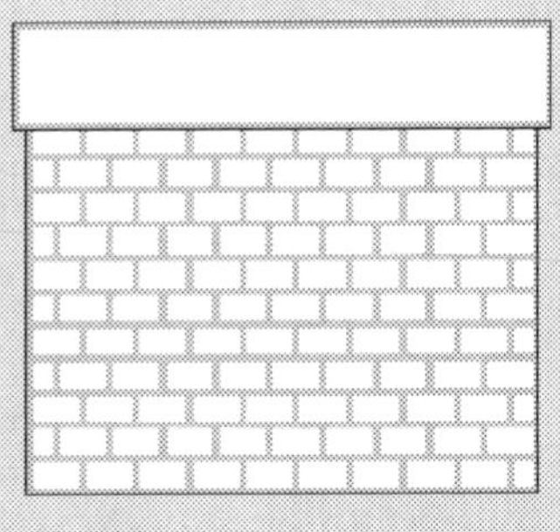

Because they lead my people astray, saying,
"Peace," when there is no peace, And
because, when a flimsy wall is built, they
cover it with whitewash,
Therefore tell those who cover it with
whitewash that it is going to fall.
Rain will come in torrents, and I will send hailstones hurtling down,
and violent winds will burst forth.
When the wall collapses, will people not ask you,
'Where is the whitewash you covered it with?'
Therefore this is what the Sovereign LORD says:
'In my wrath I will unleash a violent wind,
and in my anger hailstones
And torrents of rain will fall with destructive fury.
I will tear down the wall you have covered with whitewash
And will level it to the ground so that its foundation will be laid bare.
When it falls, you will be destroyed in it;
And you will know that I am the LORD.
So I will spend my wrath against the wall
And against those who covered it with whitewash.'
I will say to you,
'The wall is gone and so are those who whitewashed it,
Those prophets of Israel
Who prophesied to Jerusalem
And saw visions of peace for her when there was no peace,'
Declares the Sovereign LORD
Ezekiel 13:9-13 (Today's NIV)

PROPHETIC DECLARATIONS

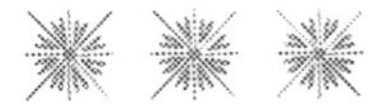

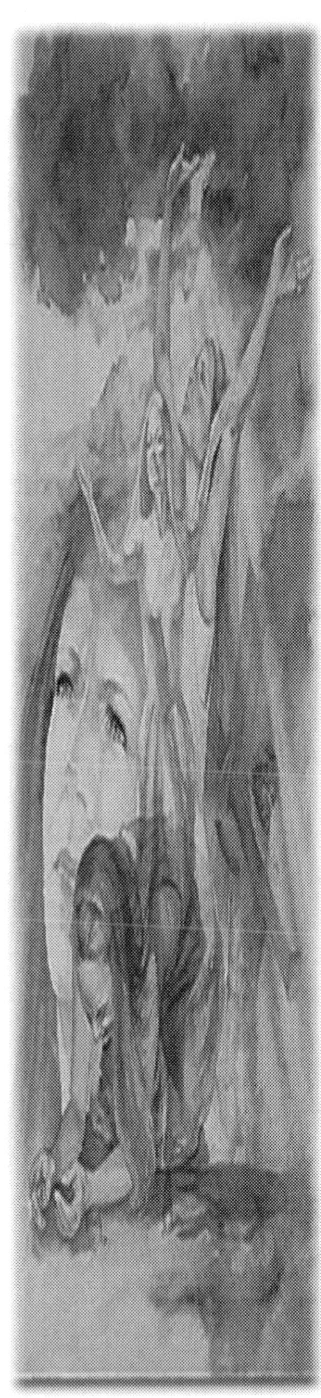

"W.O.M.B" Women Of Multitudinous Birthings

❋ ❋ ❋

Before every great move of God is manifested throughout this realm, there is a womb within the Body of Christ that incubates that promise from conception up to the place where we see the manifestation. (Giving birth)

That promise (Seed), be it the promise made first to Abraham and Sarah concerning the seed that will be multiplied as the sand of the sea shore, ushering in the call of Rachel and Leah giving birth to the twelve tribes of Israel—God's chosen People, or the seed given to Hanna bringing forth the Child Samuel known as the season and timing of God's chosen Prophets and Kings, or to the virgin Mary, heralding the coming Messiah and giving birth to the Child of God, the one who came to be our Saviour and who is our Saviour.

Today that seed is sown within the body of Christ to bring forth the manifestation of the Power of God in this end time.

The whole creation is groaning, waiting in expectation for the manifestation of the sons of God as declared in Romans 8:19-23, in bringing deliverance from all sin which brings forth death to our spirit soul and body.

This groan, which is the prayers of the travailing saints are joined with the unutterable longing of the Spirit of God in unison, for the arising of God's deliverers. These "sons of God" will move in the *fullness* of the anointing, the fullness of the gifts and the fullness of the power of God. The greater works promised by Jesus will be done by the sons of God. The "works that He did" have in measure been done by believers during the church age, miracles have happened. The sick have been healed, the blind see, the deaf have heard and the dumb spoke.

Many Christians have embraced the word of God and by faith "all things are possible to them that believe" but the "greater works" have been reserved for this season, for this time. The "sons of God" will walk in unlimited power and authority. The most glorious times in the world's history lies before us. The visible glory of the Lord will appear upon multitudes of people, and power will flow out from them to convict, deliver and transform all who come into their presence. The cloud and pillar of fire that hovered over Israel in the wilderness will not even compare to the intense presence of the Lord in these days. God Himself will be personal and intimate with His people. This is where we are in this season of Gods timing saints of "The Most High God," Let us embrace His Presence and Let us embrace His Person.

People of God, we are impregnated with that seed in this hour and it is time for its delivery. We have got to give birth in this hour.

I hear the Lord say:

> *"The whole creation groans, even the earth has opened her womb to give birth to the manifestation of the power of God. The womb of the earth is like the situation with Pharaoh, you have to receive storms, pestilences and even plaques sometimes to get her to release my people*

Come Into My Chambers!

"You have invited a friend of yours (The world)

To usher you into my bedchambers,
One who could not prepare you for such an entrance,
One who will never be able to penetrate, playing around with her fingers.

You have great difficulties in totally submitting to Me
You know that I am interested in coming into a complete Relationship with you,
Yet you're pulling away

She called to confirm that everything was in order, but you did not come in.
You were left with deep thoughts, questioning yourself as to why you could not allow yourself to come in with Me
You were left wondering; why it is that you could not fall in love with me totally
You are very cautious, not so much rebellious, but cautious".

. . . . And I cried: "Lord, I was afraid of allowing you to become intimate with me. I was hurt so many times before and I really do not want to feel any more pain. Everything about you is awesome, and you're very beautiful, but I really cannot afford to give up my soul, I am very comfortable the way I am, and in the position I am in".

"Do you know that this whole scene exemplifies what is happening within the body, representing the level of our intimacy?

But, I do love you, I died for you, come into my bedchambers, I love you—come in with me, and you will never be the same again. Come!"